Karoly Nyisztor

DESIGN PATTERNS IN SWIFT 5

I0394084

LEARN HOW TO IMPLEMENT SOFTWARE DESIGN PATTERNS USING SWIFT 5.
ELEVATE YOUR CODING SKILLS.

For the visionaries
who believe that Swift programming is not just about solving problems,
but about doing so with grace, precision, and artistry.

Contents

1. INTRODUCTION

1.1 What's Covered in this Book?

Since the rules of software development are not carved in stone, we have some flexibility when it comes to designing and implementing software systems.

The chosen approach might depend on personal taste, the abilities of the team, and other variables. However, not all designs are equally effective. Eventually, we'll find out whether a software solution is robust and future-proof—but we don't have to find out the truth the hard way.

Luckily, there are battle-proven best practices and principles known as software development patterns that have been used for decades. We do not have to reinvent the wheel: by understanding and applying these design patterns, we can ensure that our software gets built on a solid foundation.

This book is an overview of software design patterns and the way they are implemented using Swift 5, Apple's latest iteration of their popular programming language. We'll talk about the benefits of understanding and applying the design patterns, the value they provide, and also about their limitations.

Then, we delve into creational design patterns: the Singleton, the Prototype, the Factory Method, the Builder, and the Abstract Factory design patterns.

We're going to take a closer look at structural design patterns; we will first discuss the Adapter, the Bridge, the Decorator, the Composite, the Facade, the Flyweight, and we will finish with the Proxy pattern.

In the final part of this book, we will discuss behavioral design patterns. We'll start with the Chain of Responsibility, and we will finish with the State design pattern. There are ten behavioral patterns, so this is going to be massive.

For each design pattern, we will discuss the following:

- → When to use the given Pattern
- → How can it be implemented using Swift
- → Challenges and pitfalls

Throughout the book, I provide coding examples that can be applied in real-world situations.

My goal is to introduce you to software design patterns and the way they can be implemented in modern Swift. Upon completing this book, you'll be able to apply these patterns when building apps and frameworks using Swift.

1.2 Prerequisites

This is an intermediate programming book that aims to deepen your knowledge of design patterns and coding best practices.

I'm going to explain all the concepts and will provide thorough explanations regarding implementation details and about the sample code we use throughout this book.

However, since we delve into more advanced topics, prior knowledge of software development and some experience in Xcode and Swift programming are required.

We're going to work with protocols, classes, value types, and dispatch queues. We'll use Xcode to create playgrounds and iOS projects. If you're not familiar with these concepts, you should start studying the basics of Swift and iOS/macOS development.

To implement the exercises in this book, you'll need XCode 12.5 or newer. You can download Xcode for free from the Mac App Store.

2. DESIGN PATTERNS: BENEFITS AND LIMITATIONS

2.1 The History of Software Design Patterns

As software developers, we need to solve various problems. That's been the case since we started working with computers, and the situation won't change anytime soon. As you might've experienced, we often encounter similar or even the very same challenges.

Over time, software engineers have developed solutions and best practices to solve these recurring problems. Every company, team, or individual could come up with the "next best solution." The lack of a standardized way to address these common challenges leads to slightly different approaches to the same issue.

In 1994, four authors published a book called "Design Patterns - Elements of Reusable Object-Oriented Software."

> Because the name of the book is quite long, it became known as the "book by the gang of four."

The authors are Erich Gamma, Ralph Johnson, Richard Helm, and John Vlissides—also known as the Gang of Four (GoF). Their goal was to standardize some of the already identified best-practices.

The term "design pattern" became the official name for a strategy to deal with a common software development problem. The most important design patterns originate from this classic book written decades ago. These patterns are still used today in modern software development, and every object-oriented programming language provides the means to implement them.

Design patterns—as we call them today—are the result of a long process of evolution. They provide proven solutions to certain problems faced during software development. Understanding these patterns helps inexperienced developers to learn software design in an easy, fast and secure way.

We can use design patterns with any object-oriented programming language. Moreover, many modern programming languages and frameworks have integrated the GoF patterns. We don't have to write additional code to support, say, the Iterator or the Observer.

Swift provides many advanced language features and constructs: type extensions, lazy initialization, and predefined protocols that let us adopt and integrate design patterns into our projects easily. We're going to talk about these and many more in the upcoming chapters.

The goal of this book is to help you identify and apply the patterns you need to address specific problems. Also, you will receive Swift implementations that you can reuse in your projects.

2.2 The Benefits of Design Patterns

You may ask: What's wrong with figuring out the solution ourselves? What's so special about software design patterns?

First, these best practices are proven to work. They have been used in countless projects across several platforms. These design patterns have been refined over the decades and adapted to various programming languages.

Instead of coming up with a custom solution, you can spend that time implementing new features or improving the quality of your project.

Moreover, by applying time-tested design patterns, it will be easier to extend, modify, fix, and test your code.

That's because design patterns make you think outside of the box. You're not only focusing on the very problem you're trying to solve, but you also need to factor in concepts like loose coupling, separation of concerns, single responsibility, data hiding, and polymorphism.

To sum up, design patterns help us create software systems that are easier to maintain, extend, or enhance. By avoiding unnecessary changes in our code base, we reduce the chances of introducing new bugs. We can also save time that can be instead spent on developing essential features and improving the reliability of our project.

That doesn't mean that design patterns solve every problem and automatically eliminate all possible bugs. In reality, they come with their own challenges and limitations, too.

2.3 Pitfalls and Limitations

Despite all the benefits, there are also some risks and limitations involved in using design patterns.

The human factor

Getting your team members to see the value in design patterns can be tricky at times. You should be able to explain the benefits of introducing a specific design pattern. For that, you need to understand how the pattern works and how it can be applied in that particular programming language.

Skills required

Applying a design pattern requires a certain level of expertise. Some developers might need additional time to understand and implement the patterns correctly. The ramp-up period will introduce delays and more bugs than usual, which in turn leads to friction within the team and increased resistance to adopting the design patterns.

Not one-size-fits-all solutions

Another aspect is that design patterns are generic by nature. That is, we usually can't just apply them as is to every situation. A design pattern needs to address a family of similar problems, which may become an impediment when trying to solve a specific issue. So, keep in mind that it requires creativity and tweaking to adapt a pattern to fit the project's unique needs.

Overuse

Before implementing a design pattern, ask yourself if it is really necessary. If the problem you are trying to solve is simple and isolated, and you won't need to touch that part of your code again, introducing a design pattern may be overcomplicating things. Instead, opt for a simpler solution that gets the job done. Don't make your life harder than it needs to be.

> Don't introduce a design pattern just for the sake of it.

Design patterns can help us build better software systems. However, it takes time and practice to apply them effectively.

2.4 Classification of Design Patterns

The Gang of Four (GoF) grouped software design patterns into three distinct categories:

→ creational

→ structural

→ behavioral

The following diagram provides an overview of the GoF software design patterns organized by categories:

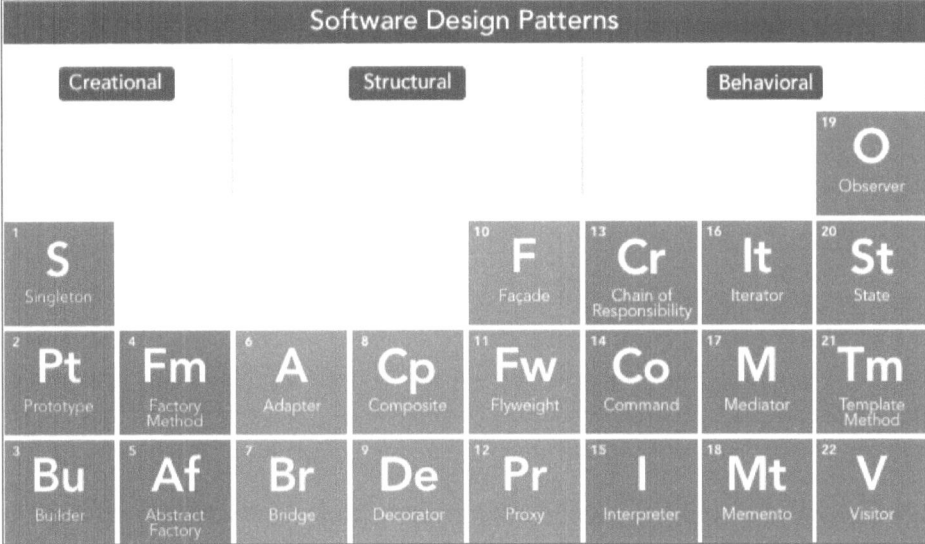

Creational Design Patterns

Creational design patterns are about object creation, and their purpose is to separate the usage of an object from its instantiation. Thus, we don't expose the creation details to the users of our objects.

As a consequence, we simplify the usage of our objects and reduce the coupling within our system. We'll discuss the following creational design patterns:

→ the Singleton

→ the Prototype

→ the Builder

→ the Factory Method

→ the Abstract Factory

The Singleton design pattern is useful if we need to ensure that there's only one instance of a type. We'll delve into implementation details, and address the most significant challenge that arises while working with this pattern: ensuring thread safety.

The Prototype is concerned with the cloning of objects. We'll talk about cloning value and reference types, and also about some pitfalls we may encounter while implementing this pattern.

The Builder separates the creation of objects from their configuration. It simplifies the creation of instances that need many default values that don't frequently change when creating new objects.

The Factory Method lets us create objects without knowing their exact type. This design pattern exposes only the protocol or the top level class to callers, thus reducing dependencies within the system.

The Abstract Factory provides an abstraction for creating families of related or dependent objects. We're going to refactor a tightly coupled system and remove the unnecessary dependencies.

Structural Design Patterns

We rarely encounter isolated objects in real-world software systems. Structural design patterns aim to compose objects and classes into larger structures or to achieve new functionality while keeping the design flexible and efficient.

We're going to explore the most frequently used structural design patterns:

- → the Adapter
- → the Decorator
- → the Façade
- → the Flyweight
- → and the Proxy pattern

The Adapter pattern is a useful strategy for dealing with incompatible interfaces, a common challenge when working with legacy systems.

The Decorator pattern allows us to add functionality to an object dynamically without modifying its source code. It is a useful technique when we cannot or do not want to alter the implementation of a type.

The Façade is a straightforward and easy-to-implement design pattern that shines when it comes to simplifying the usage of complex interfaces.

The Flyweight design pattern can come in handy when the memory usage of our programs surges due to a plethora of similar objects.

The last structural pattern we'll discuss is the Proxy. Acting as a surrogate, it intercepts all access to the cloaked object. The Proxy is a versatile pattern that can be used to defer expensive instantiations, protect sensitive resources, or postpone time-consuming operations until they are actually needed.

Behavioral Design Patterns

Behavioral design patterns are concerned with how objects exchange information with each other without adding unnecessary dependencies.

Behavioral design patterns are concerned with the interaction between the objects that form a software system.

We'll delve into the following behavioral patterns:

→ Chain of Responsibility

→ Iterator

→ Observer

→ State

Even if you haven't studied design patterns before, you've been relying on the Chain of Responsibility, as it provides crucial functionality in iOS, macOS, watchOS, and tvOS.

Next, we'll delve into the Iterator design pattern. This pattern is used to navigate through the elements of a sequence without exposing the underlying data structure to the user. Whenever we use a for-in loop, we rely on the Iterator pattern.

The Observer pattern allows objects to subscribe to notifications without being tightly coupled to the sender.

The State design pattern helps us to replace complex conditional statements that tend to spread across our code base with elegant, object-oriented state machines.

We'll use modern Swift language features to implement each pattern while also touching upon best practices and things to consider. Let's dig in!

3. THE SINGLETON

3.1 Overview

Let's start our study of creational design patterns with the Singleton, a pattern renowned for its utility and potential for misuse.

Purpose

The Singleton design pattern's primary goal is to provide a globally accessible, shared instance of a given class.

This pattern can serve you well if you need to provide a unified access point to a unique resource such as a database controller or a network manager that can be accessed and used throughout your application.

The shared UserDefaults object—UserDefaults.standard—or the shared file manager object—FileManager.default—are good examples of commonly used singletons on the Apple platform.

Here's the UML representation of the Singleton:

Singleton
+shared
-init()

Note that the init() method is private, effectively preventing any external instantiation of the class. The Singleton needs to provide a global point of access to the shared instance. Clients can access the singleton instance solely via this access point, which can be a static type property or a class method.

This approach guarantees that the Singleton class has exactly one instance.

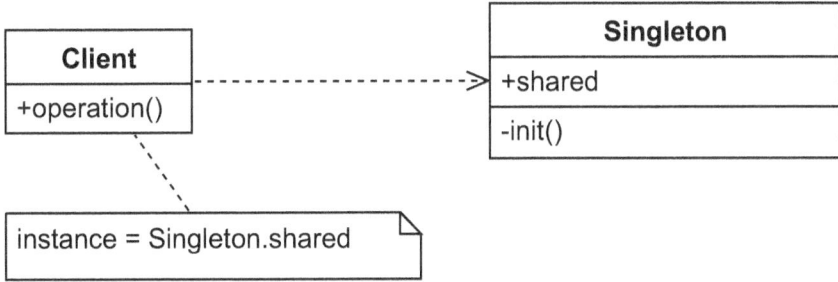

A value type can't implement the Singleton design pattern, because copying creates an independent instance. Thus, we can't prevent the creation of multiple objects of the same type.

Also, a Singleton class must not adopt the NSCopying protocol. Otherwise, clients can create copies, which defeats the purpose of the Singleton.

Pitfalls

Despite its clear utility, the Singleton pattern's application is not without its pitfalls.

Treating Singletons as global multipurpose containers is a classic example of abusing this pattern.

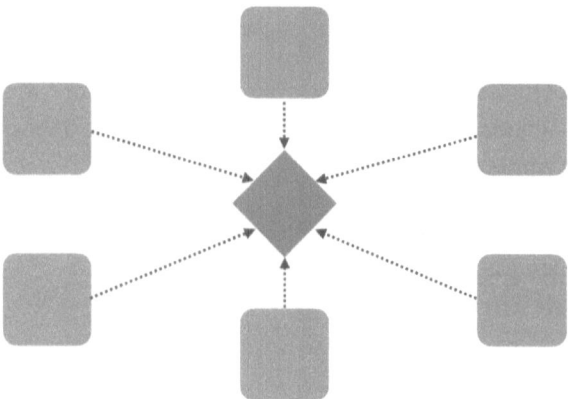

Using Singletons as a global shared state goes against the Single Responsibility Principle, which asserts that each type should have one, well-defined responsibility. This principle is one of the five fundamental object-oriented design principles known as SOLID principles.

Another issue with Singletons is that once you start using them, they tend to spread across your codebase. Eventually, you lose track of the objects that depend on the singletons.

These dependencies are hidden since you don't have to pass the singleton to a method, or an initializer, or assign it to a property of a type to use it. Thus, the system may appear less coupled than it truly is.

However, changes to the singleton will trigger widespread modifications in the code of seemingly unrelated components. This ripple effect is quite a common problem in projects that rely heavily on singletons and global instances.

On top of these object-oriented design concerns, ensuring thread safety within a Singleton without compromising performance requires careful consideration and implementation.

In the following sections, we'll delve into the implementation nuances of the Singleton pattern, addressing these concerns and demonstrating best practices to maintain thread safety and performance integrity.

3.2 Implementing a Singleton

Let's implement the Singleton design pattern in Swift. We're going to build an app called AppSettingsDemo.

Start by opening Xcode and create a new SwiftUI application. Name it AppSettingsDemo. We'll use SwiftUI for the user interface, and skip tests by leaving "Include Tests" unchecked. Xcode creates the project and it generates some initial boilerplate code. We're not interested in the preview so let's choose Show Editor Only—or simply press Command-Enter.

Next, add a new Swift file to your project. Right-click on the top project folder in the project navigator, choose Swift for the file type and call it AppSettings.

In the AppSettings file, we declare the AppSettings class. Make it final to prevent the creation of subclasses:

```
final public class AppSettings {}
```

Our next step is to prevent external instantiation of the AppSettings class. Make the init() method private:

```
    private init() {}
```

Now, we expose a static property named 'shared' for accessing the Singleton instance:

```
    public static let shared = AppSettings()
```

Swift ensures that static properties like 'shared' are accessed safely across multiple threads.

In the AppSettings class, we'll store and retrieve application data using a private dictionary named 'settings':

```
    private var settings: [String: Any] = [:]
```

For managing this data, define a set(value:, forKey:) method. It's public and accepts any type as its argument, with the key as a String:

```
    public func set(value: Any, forKey key: String) {
        settings[key] = value
    }
```

Also, implement the objectForKey method to return a value for a given key. Since the key might not exist, the method returns an optional:

```
public func object(forKey key: String) -> Any? {
    return settings[key]
}
```

Lastly, add a reset method to clear the settings dictionary:

```
public func reset() {
    settings.removeAll()
}
```

With these steps, we have a basic Singleton pattern implementation with some basic functionality.

However, it has a serious flaw: it's not thread safe! To illustrate the issue, we're going to do some testing.

3.3 Concurrency Issues

We just implemented our Singleton, but is it ready for production? Let's see what happens if we start using it from multiple threads.

In our SwiftUI AppSettingsDemo project, we're going to add some keys and values to the AppSettings object. We'll keep it simple for this demo and add the required code directly in the ContentView.

We can use the onAppear modifier in our ContentView to trigger our test code before the view appears.

We'll use a for-in loop to generate 100 keys and their matching values. Define a constant count and assign it the value 100:

```
struct ContentView: View {
    var body: some View {
        VStack {
            Image(systemName: "globe")
                .imageScale(.large)
                .foregroundStyle(.tint)
            Text("Hello, world!")
        }
        .padding()
        .onAppear {
            // Add key-value pairs to AppSettings
            let count = 100


        }
    }
}
```

In each iteration, add a new key-value pair to the shared AppSettings instance. The value is the index, and the key is its string representation:

```
.onAppear {
    // Add key-value pairs to AppSettings
    let count = 100
    for index in 0..<count {
        AppSettings.shared.set(value: index, forKey:
String(index))
    }
}
}
}
}
```

Now, let's retrieve the values we just set. To simulate a multi-threaded environment, we'll use DispatchQueue.concurrentPerform() method, implementing a parallel for-loop:

```
        .onAppear {
            // Add key-value pairs to AppSettings
            let count = 100
            for index in 0..<count {
                AppSettings.shared.set(value: index, forKey:
String(index))
            }
            // Retrieve values concurrently
            DispatchQueue.concurrentPerform(iterations: count) {
index in
                if let n = AppSettings.shared.object(forKey:
String(index)) as? Int {
                    print(n)
                }
            }
        }
    }
}
```

If we run the app now, the console will fill with random numbers, showing the values were retrieved concurrently.

```
            // Reset the singleton
            AppSettings.shared.reset()
```

We'll use DispatchQueue.concurrentPerform() again to concurrently update the singleton:

```
            // Concurrently update the singleton
            DispatchQueue.concurrentPerform(iterations: count) {
index in
                print("Iteration index \(index)")
                AppSettings.shared.set(value: index, forKey:
String(index))
            }
```

Rerunning the app, we might see it crash. To investigate the cause, we can use the Thread Sanitizer in Xcode.

The Thread Sanitizer is a built-in diagnostic tool that lets us analyze threading issues. It's inactive by default, so we need to enable it. I edit the project's scheme and select the Thread Sanitizer option from the Diagnostics section for the Run action.

Let's rerun the app. The ThreadSanitizer message in the console indicates that we're dealing with a concurrent access issue.

```
SUMMARY: ThreadSanitizer: Swift access race
...
AppSettingsDemo.AppSettings.set(value: Any, forKey: Swift.String)
-> ()+0x100
```

The crash occurs while updating the AppSettings dictionary. Neither dictionaries nor arrays are thread-safe by default. Accessing and modifying a dictionary from multiple threads can lead to data corruption and crashes.

Next, we'll look into making our singleton thread-safe.

3.4 Ensuring Thread-Safety with GCD

We've seen the issues that arise when multiple threads access and modify a dictionary at the same time. Now, let's make our Singleton thread safe to prevent these problems.

Ensuring thread safety in our Singleton, especially in a multithreaded environment, is crucial. For our AppSettings Singleton, we need to guard against concurrent writes or simultaneous reads and writes to the dictionary. This means synchronizing access to the set(value:, forKey:) and object(forKey:) methods.

We'll use Grand Central Dispatch (GCD) and a serial queue to synchronize access to the internal storage dictionary. Tasks in a serial queue execute one at a time, ensuring each task starts only after the previous one finishes.

Here's how we can implement this in our SwiftUI AppSettingsDemo project:

First, create a serial queue in the AppSettings class:

```
private let serialQueue = DispatchQueue(label: "serialQueue")
```

Next, we modify the set method to serialize access:

```
public func set(value: Any, forKey key: String) {
    serialQueue.sync {
        settings[key] = value
    }
}
```

This setup ensures that if multiple threads call set(value:, forKey:) concurrently, the tasks in the serial queue are executed sequentially.

We apply the same synchronization approach in the object(forKey:) method:

```
public func object(forKey key: String) -> Any? {
    var result: Any?

    serialQueue.sync {
        result = settings[key]
    }
    return result
}
```

We need to introduce a new variable that represents the result.

```
public func object(forKey key: String) -> Any? {
    var result: Any?
    serialQueue.sync {
        result = settings[key]
    }
    return result
}
```

We'll set its value in the serialQueue's sync closure. And finally, let's return the result.

```
public func object(forKey key: String) -> Any? {
    var result: Any?

    serialQueue.sync {
        result = settings[key]
    }
    return result
}
```

Using the same serial queue for both methods ensures synchronous execution, preventing data retrieval while another thread modifies the dictionary.

Now, let's test the updated Singleton in our SwiftUI app. Run the app with the

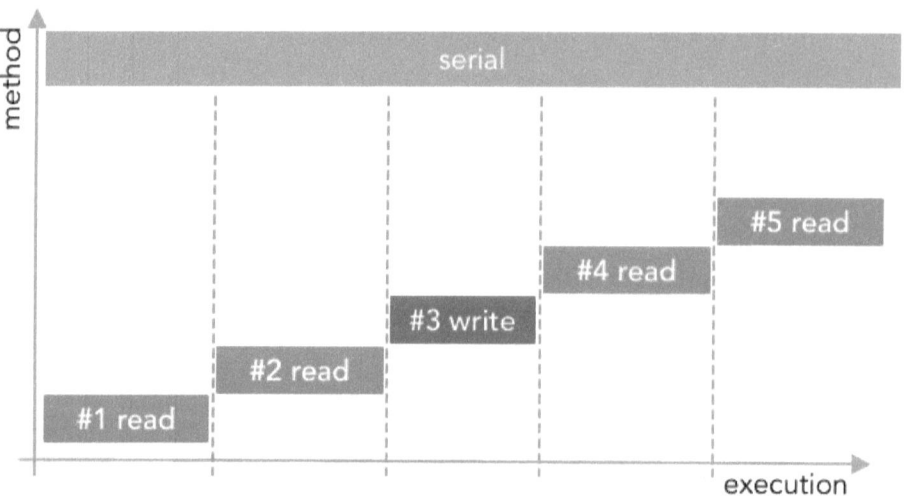

same concurrent read and write tests as before.

No matter how many times we try, this version won't crash like the initial code. This confirms that our Singleton is now thread-safe.

This is a great improvement! However, there's still room for optimization, such as implementing a "readers-writer lock" technique for better performance.

3.5 Optimizing for Speed: Readers-Writer Lock

So far, in our SwiftUI AppSettingsDemo, we've implemented a singleton class for storing and retrieving values based on unique keys and addressed concurrency issues.

To further improve performance, we'll implement a technique known as the readers/writer lock. We initially made the AppSettings class thread-safe using a serial queue, but this approach has its limitations due to the blocking nature of serial queues.

Recall that reading values simultaneously from the AppSettings singleton doesn't pose concurrency hazards. Race conditions primarily occur during concurrent modifications. In theory, we could allow concurrent read operations, provided no writes are happening. This would enhance performance in multi-threaded read scenarios.

However, we can't undo the changes we've made to serialize the access to the object(forKey:) method. We still need to synchronize read and write operations to prevent race conditions.

Grand Central Dispatch offers a solution for this classic 'Readers-Writers Problem' in the form of dispatch barriers.

Let's apply this in our project. In the AppSettings file, replace the serial queue with a concurrent queue:

```
    private let concurrentQueue = DispatchQueue(label: "concurrent-
Queue", attributes: .concurrent)
```

Next, we'll refactor the set(value:, forKey:) method to use the concurrentQueue with a dispatch barrier: We'll call its async method because we don't need to wait until the block finishes.

Note that we use a dispatch barrier in the flags argument. The barrier turns the concurrent queue into a serial one temporarily. As a consequence, no other thread can modify the internal dictionary while this block is executing.

```
    public func set(value: Any, forKey key: String) {
        concurrentQueue.async(flags: .barrier) {
            self.settings[key] = value
        }
    }
```

The barrier ensures exclusive access for the write operation, temporarily making the concurrent queue serial.

Let's also refactor the object(forKey:) method to utilize the concurrentQueue:

```
public func object(forKey key: String) -> Any? {
    var result: Any?

    concurrentQueue.sync {
        result = settings[key]
    }
    return result
}
```

With this enhancement, read operations can execute in parallel when the barrier is not active, potentially speeding up the application in certain scenarios.

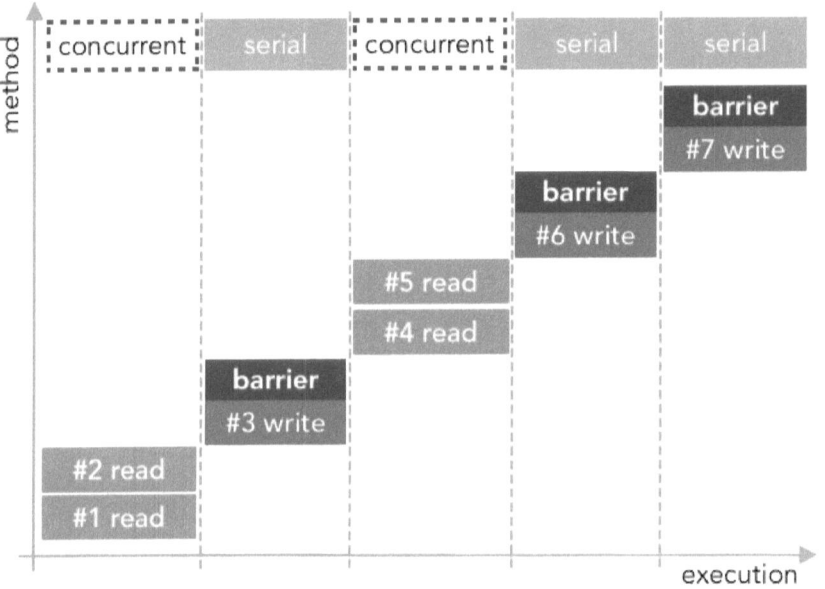

We implemented a dispatch-barrier-based readers-writer lock. Our Singleton is not only thread-safe but also optimized for performance.

3.6 Conclusion

The singleton pattern is easy to understand. The aim is to create a class which can have exactly one instance.

Sounds easy, right? But as we've seen, the devil is in the details.

Enforce Unique Instance

First off, we've got to make sure that our Singleton really is a Singleton. This means no copying or cloning. In Swift, we stick to classes for this—value types just won't do, as they get copied around. And remember, Singleton classes must not adopt the NSCopying protocol.

Ensure Thread Safety

Then, there's the matter of thread safety. Singletons might be used concurrently, so making them thread-safe is non-negotiable. We've navigated through serial queues and dispatch barriers to achieve this.

Adhere to the Single Responsibility Principle

Singletons - just like any other class - must have a well-defined responsibility. Misusing the Singleton as a global container is a common problem.

Be Aware of Tight-coupling Risks

And let's not forget about dependencies and coupling. Singletons can create hidden dependencies and cause tight coupling within a system.

Coming up next, we're going to explore the Prototype design pattern.

4. THE PROTOTYPE

4.1 Overview

When we find ourselves frequently initializing complex objects, it's time to consider the Prototype design pattern.

This pattern is particularly useful when creating instances of a type from scratch is resource-intensive or inefficient.

Think of nearly identical objects that require time-consuming initialization, which involves, say, fetching data from the file system, executing complex validation steps, and performing extensive calculations.

Purpose

The Prototype pattern solves the problem of extensive repeated initializations by cloning a pre-existing object.

It's like having an instance that we can quickly replicate. This approach improves efficiency while simplifying the creation of complex objects, making your code easier to manage and maintain.

In the UML diagram for the Prototype pattern, we start with a prototype instance created as usual. Every subsequent instance is then created by cloning this prototype using its clone() method.

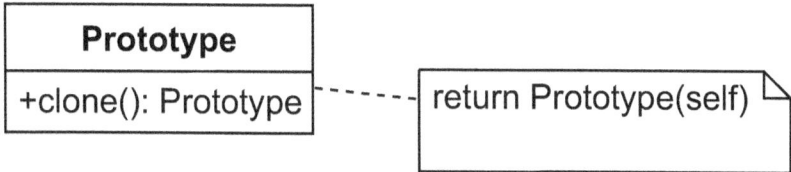

We can improve our design further by removing direct coupling between the client and the Prototype object's concrete type. To achieve this, we define a Prototype interface that declares the clone() method. Clients can interact with the Prototype interface to clone objects without knowing their concrete types, leveraging polymorphism.

Pitfalls

While the Prototype pattern is convenient, there are specific nuances we should consider.

Value types like structs, enums, and tuples are automatically copied on assignment, giving us prototype behavior for free.

However, cloning reference types—or value types with class-type properties—is more complex and requires a deep understanding of shallow versus deep copying. Implementing copy behavior for such instances and their properties can be challenging and may lead to extensive changes throughout your codebase.

Additionally, we need to ensure that the clones are independent. Changes to a clone should not impact the original prototype object or other clones.

The benefits and applications of the Prototype pattern will become evident as we delve further into the implementation specifics using Swift. In our upcoming section, we'll explore the differences between copying value and reference types.

4.2 Copying Value Types

In Swift, value types are copied upon assignment. Thus, we get the prototype behavior without additional coding.

Let's start with an Xcode playground project called PrototypeDemo.

Define a struct called `Contact`. Add two properties of type `String`, `firstName` and `lastName`.

```
struct Contact {
    var firstName: String
    var lastName: String
}
```

Swift defines the `String` as a value type:

```
public struct String {...}
```

Note that all other built-in numeric types, Booleans, enumerations, collections, and tuples are implemented as structures. Thus, whenever you assign a built-in type to a variable, its value gets copied and used to create the clone.

Next, create a `Contact` instance.

```
var john = Contact(firstName: "John", lastName: "Appleseed")
```

Create another variable called 'bob,' and assign the first instance to it:

```
var bob = john
```

Finally, print the description of both instances to the console:

```
print("\(john),\n\(bob)")
```

Run the playground. The console shows the following:

```
Contact(firstName: "John", lastName: "Appleseed"),
Contact(firstName: "John", lastName: "Appleseed")
```

The clone and the original instance share the same values for their `firstName` and `lastName` properties. However, `Contact` is a value type; therefore, the memory addresses of the two objects are different. We can prove it by updating the properties of the clone:

```
bob.firstName = "Bob"
bob.lastName = "Burger"
```

Again, let's print the description of both instances:

```
print("\(john),\n\(bob)")
```

Here's the output of the second print statement:

```
Contact(firstName: "John", lastName: "Appleseed"),
Contact(firstName: "Bob", lastName: "Burger")
```

Indeed, the two instances are different.

Whenever we assign an object of a value type to another object, its value gets copied and used to initialize the clone. However, changing the clone (the bob instance) does not affect the original instance (john).

Reference types behave differently. Assigning an instance of a class type to another instance produces two references that point to the same object. Implementing the prototype behavior requires additional coding, as we'll see in the upcoming sections.

4.3 Copying Reference Types

Value types are perfect candidates for the prototype pattern. We get the required behavior without writing a single line of code.

Reference types are different: if we assign an instance of a class to another instance of the same type, they will point to the same object. That's the expected behavior for reference types. Changing any of them will affect the contents of the other one, too.

Open the PrototypeDemo playground project and add a new playground page called CloningReferenceTypes.

This time we'll declare a class instead of a structure. The Contact class has two properties named firstName and lastName.

```
class Contact {
    var firstName: String
    var lastName: String
}
```

We need to add an initializer, too:

```
    init(firstName: String, lastName: String) {
        self.firstName = firstName
        self.lastName = lastName
    }
```

Add CustomStringConvertible protocol conformance to the Contact class using a type extension. CustomStringConvertible declares the description property that allows us to provide a human-friendly description for our class.

```
extension Contact: CustomStringConvertible {}
```

The implementation returns the firstName and the lastName as the object's description:

```
extension Contact: CustomStringConvertible {
    public var description: String {
        "Contact(firstName: \"\(firstName)\", lastName: \"\(last-
Name)\")"
    }
}
```

Create an instance, and let's call it john:

```
var john = Contact(firstName: "John", lastName: "Appleseed")
```

And I assign it to another variable called bob:

```
var bob = john
```

If we print the description of the two instances, we'll see that they share the same values:

```
print("\(john), \(bob)")
```

```
The output will be:
```

```
Contact(firstName: "John", lastName: "Appleseed"),
Contact(firstName: "John", lastName: "Appleseed")
```

Now let's check what happens if we update the second instance's firstName and lastName property:

```
bob.firstName = "Bob"
bob.lastName = "Burger"
```

Again, we print the description of the two objects to the console:

```
print("\(john), \(bob)")
```

Here's the console output. It shows that both objects were updated:

```
Contact(firstName: "Bob", lastName: "Burger"),
Contact(firstName: "Bob", lastName: "Burger")
```

Unlike value types, reference types are not copied; both Contact objects refer to the same shared instance.

That's precisely how reference type instances are supposed to behave. When we assign an object of a class to a new variable, both will point to the same memory address. Thus, we don't actually have two different objects, but two names—or references—for the same instance.

Implementing the prototype pattern for reference types requires some extra coding, as we'll see in the next section.

4.4 Cloning Reference Types

As we just saw, reference types don't get the copy behavior automatically. To implement the prototype pattern, reference types need to adopt the NSCopying protocol.

The NSCopying protocol declares the copy(with:) method, which lets us create clones of a given object.

Let's add NSCopying conformance to the Contact type.

```
class Contact: NSCopying {...}
```

Next, implement the copy(with:) method.

```
class Contact: NSCopying {
    public func copy(with zone: NSZone? = nil) -> Any {
        Contact(firstName: self.firstName, lastName: self.lastName)
    }
}
```

The method returns a new instance and passes the property values of the object to the newly created one.

It is not possible to overload the default assignment operator (=). So, we must explicitly call the copy() method during assignment.

```
var bob = john.copy() as! Contact
```

The copy() method returns a result of type Any. Thus, we must cast the result to the actual type.

Now the clone and the prototype point to different objects. Changing one instance does not affect the other one.

Let's run the playground—here's the console output:

```
Contact(firstName: "John", lastName: "Appleseed"),
Contact(firstName: "Bob", lastName: "Burger")
```

Indeed, the two instances now point to two different objects. Although we can't overload the assignment operator, we can provide a more elegant solution. Let's define a clone() method:

```
class Contact: NSCopying {
    // ...
    func clone() -> Contact {
        self.copy() as! Contact
```

```
        }
}
```

The method's return type is `Contact`. It simply invokes the `copy(with:)` method and performs the required type conversion. We can now use a shorter syntax to clone `Contact` objects:

```
var bob = john.clone()
```

The copying of class instances is not impossible, but it requires some additional coding. Besides, we can't overload the assignment operator to make it work just as it does for value types.

Although you can implement the copy behavior, Swift wants to make reference semantics clear.

4.5 Shallow Copy vs. Deep Copy

Let's talk about shallow and deep copying. These concepts are related to copying objects which contain pointers to other objects.

I'm going to show you how to copy the real contents instead of just copying pointer values. To illustrate the issue first, we'll add a new property of type `Address` to our `Contact` class.

To recap, our `Contact` class already implements the prototype pattern so that we can correctly copy it when needed. So far, it only has value type properties, which are ultimately copied correctly.

`Address` is a class with three properties of type `String`: `street`, `city`, and `zip`.

```
class Address {
    var street: String
    var city: String
    var zip: String
}
```

We need to implement an initializer:

```
    init(street: String, city: String, zip: String) {
        self.street = street
        self.city = city
        self.zip = zip
    }
```

The `Address` class conforms to the `CustomStringConvertible` protocol to provide a custom description.

```
extension Address: CustomStringConvertible {
    public var description: String {
        "street: \"\(street)\", city: \"\(city)\", zip: \"\
(zip)\""
    }
}
```

Let's add the address property to our `Contact` class.

```
class Contact {
    var firstName: String
    var lastName: String
    var address: String
}
```

We must make sure that the new property is initialized in the `Contact` class's `init()` method.

```
init(firstName: String, lastName: String, address: String) {
    self.firstName = firstName
    self.lastName = lastName
    self.address = address
}
```

We need to update the `copy(with:)` method, too.

```
public func copy(with zone: NSZone? = nil) -> Any {
    Contact(firstName: self.firstName, lastName: self.lastName,
address: self.address)
    }
```

And finally, let's include the address in the custom `Contact` description:

```
extension Contact: CustomStringConvertible {
    public var description: String {
        "Contact(firstName: \"\(firstName)\", lastName: \"\(last-
Name)\"), address: \"\(address)\")"
    }
}
```

Next, initialize the prototype instance:

```
var john = Contact(firstName: "John",
                   lastName: "Appleseed",
                   address: Address(street: "1, Infinite Loop",
                   city: "Cupertino",
                   zip: "95014"))
```

Then, assign the copy of the prototype object to another variable:

```
var bob = john.clone()
```

Next, we change the properties of the bob instance.

```
bob.firstName = "Bob"
bob.lastName = "Burger"
bob.address.city = "Los Angeles"
bob.address.street = "2700, N Vermont Ave"
bob.address.zip = "90027"
```

After printing the description of the two objects, we notice a weird artifact.

```
print("\(john), \(bob)")
```

Let's have a look at the console output:

```
Contact(firstName: "John", lastName: "Appleseed",
        address: "street: "2700, N Vermont Ave", city: "Los Ange-
les", zip: "90027"),
Contact(firstName: "Bob", lastName: "Burger",
        address: "street: "2700, N Vermont Ave", city: "Los Ange-
les", zip: "90027"))
```

The firstName and the lastName properties are different, as they should be, but the street, the city and the zip have changed for both objects.

That's because Address is a reference type. When we pass it to the Contact initializer in the copy(with:) method, the address object won't be copied.

```
    public func copy(with zone: NSZone? = nil) -> Any {
        Contact(firstName: self.firstName, lastName: self.lastName,
address: self.address)
    }
```

Instead, the pointer that points to the address property gets copied. That's what we call a shallow copy.
Shallow copying means that we copied the memory address of an object rather than cloning the object itself. Both Contact objects point to the same Address object.

To solve the problem, we have to ensure that the contents of the address property are copied rather than its memory address.

Since firstName and lastName are value types, they are copied correctly. We need to implement the deep copying of the address property only.

Let's change the Address class so that it adopts the NSCopying protocol.

```
class Address: NSCopying {
    public func copy(with zone: NSZone? = nil) -> Any {
        Address(street: self.street, city: self.city, zip: self.
zip)
    }
```

In the Contact class's copy(with:) method implementation, make sure that the copy of the address property is made by calling the copy() method:

```
    public func copy(with zone: NSZone? = nil) -> Any {
        Contact(firstName: self.firstName, lastName: self.lastName,
address: self.address.copy() as! Address)
    }
```

This change fixed the issue: the two objects now have different addresses:

```
Contact(firstName: "John", lastName: "Appleseed",
        address: "street: "1, Infinite Loop", city: "Cupertino",
zip: "95014""),
Contact(firstName: "Bob", lastName: "Burger",
        address: "street: "2700, N Vermont Ave", city: "Los Ange-
les", zip: "90027""))
```

Implementing deep copying for reference types can become a tedious task, as it has to cover all reference type properties.

Besides, these properties may include further class type properties and so on. We'd have to copy the entire object graph correctly by adopting the NSCopying protocol in every affected class.

4.6 Conclusion

The prototype design pattern can be effective when creating new instances of a given type is inefficient. Instead of constructing new objects, the prototype pattern creates new instances by cloning a prototype object and copying all its properties.

The copied instance is an independent object. Changing its properties must not affect the cloned object.

In Swift, value types are automatically cloned; therefore, you get the behavior required to implement the prototype pattern for free.

Classes are reference types, which are not automatically copied during assignment or when passing them to functions or methods.

A class must adopt the NSCopying protocol to implement the prototype pattern. Moreover, it is important to understand the difference between a shallow copy and a deep copy when reference types are involved:

→   A deep copy duplicates the object's properties

→   A shallow copy duplicates only the references—that is, the pointers to those objects.

Consider the entire object hierarchy that you are cloning and not just the top one on which you call the copy method. You must carefully decide for each reference type property whether a shallow copy is sufficient or if you need a deep copy instead.

5. THE BUILDER

5.1 Overview

The Builder separates the construction of complex objects from their representation. The benefit of this separation is that clients require less knowledge about the default configuration values.

This design pattern can be applied when the initialization of a type uses many predefined defaults that don't change often.

Purpose

To understand the essence of the Builder pattern, let's have a look at a real-life example: an online store that sells laptops. The store offers three configurations:

→ The Budget model is right for most basic tasks like web browsing and word processing

→ The Office configuration is perfect for remote work

→ The High-End model is targeted toward gamers and people who do a lot of multimedia work

Budget
Web Browsing
Text Editing

Office
Mobile Work

High-End
Multimedia Work
Gaming

The website provides the technical specifications of each configuration:

Budget
13-inch
Intel Core i5
Intel UHD Graphics 617

Office
15-inch
Intel Core i7
Intel Iris Plus Graphics 645

High-End
15-inch
Intel Core i9
Radeon Pro Vega 20

After selecting a model, we can customize our computer. Say I picked the Budget laptop, but I need a faster processor. I can update the CPU from Intel Core i5 to Intel Core i9.

However, most customers will likely buy one of the pre-configured models and skip the customization step. Thus, they don't need to know about all the technical details such as processor and video card type.

Similarly, the Builder eliminates or reduces the amount of knowledge that the calling components need to have about the object. The default configuration values are incorporated into the Builder. Clients don't have to be aware of these values when creating instances of the given type.

Let's have a look at the UML diagram of the Builder pattern.

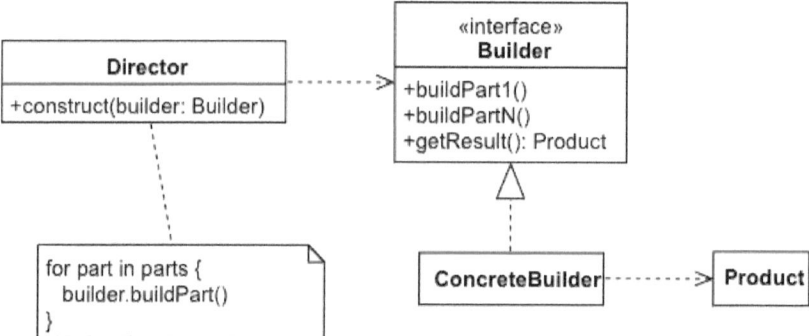

The Builder specifies the interface for creating the parts of a given product. A ConcreteBuilder implements the Builder interface and knows how to assemble a specific object. It also keeps track of the parts it creates and provides a way to retrieve the configured instance. The Director relies on the Builder to construct the object's parts.

Here's how it works. The client first instantiates a concrete builder. Then, a director object gets created that registers the builder.

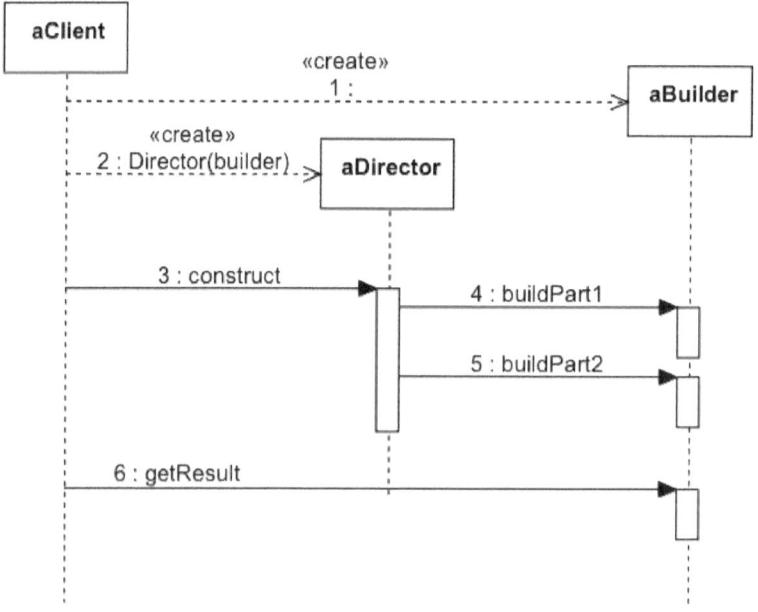

The director uses the builder to construct the parts of a complex object based on some external configuration. When the parts are ready, the client retrieves the finished product from the builder.

The director is responsible for parsing and interpreting the configuration data. The builder creates the parts that are necessary to set up the object and keeps track of the already built parts.

Pitfalls

The Builder design pattern doesn't have any drawbacks.

However, you should use it when the creation of an object requires a complex setup, with lots of different configuration values.

Also, the Builder is not what you're looking for if the configuration data differs each time you create a new object.

Next, we're going to have a look at an example that's a perfect candidate for the Builder.

5.2 Mapping the LaptopShop to Swift Code

I'm going to illustrate the problem solved by the Builder pattern through the Online Laptop Shop example.

I've gone ahead and created a playground project called LaptopShop. The Laptop.swift source file contains the definition of the Laptop class and the types used to describe its properties.

So, this is the Laptop class:

```swift
public class Laptop {
    public var size: Size
    public var processor: Processor
    public var graphics: Graphics

    public init(size: Size, processor: Processor, graphics: Graph-
ics) {
        self.size = size
        self.processor = processor
        self.graphics = graphics
    }
}
```

The class has three public properties: size, processor, and graphics. These properties let us describe the configuration shown on the website:

Budget	**Office**	**High-End**
13-inch	15-inch	15-inch
Intel Core i5	Intel Core i7	Intel Core i9
Intel UHD Graphics 617	Intel Iris Plus Graphics 645	Radeon Pro Vega 20

I also provided a custom description using a type extension that adopts the CustomStringConvertible protocol:

```swift
extension Laptop: CustomStringConvertible {
    public var description: String {
        "\(size) laptop\n\tProcessor \(processor)\n\tGraphics \
(graphics)"
    }
}
```

I defined the Size, Processor, and Graphics as enumerations that store raw String values.

The `Size` enumeration has two cases: `thirteenInch` and `fifteenInch`. The description returns the predefined raw value.

```
public enum Size: String, CustomStringConvertible {
    case thirteenInch = "13-inch"
    case fifteenInch = "15-inch"

    public var description: String {
        self.rawValue
    }
}
```

Similarly, we've got an enumeration for the `Processor`, that defines three cases: Intel Core i5, Core i7, and Core i9.

```
public enum Processor: String, CustomStringConvertible {
    case i5 = "Intel Core i5"
    case i7 = "Intel Core i7"
    case i9 = "Intel Core i9"

    public var description: String {
        self.rawValue
    }
}
```

Finally, here's the enumeration that defines the three values matching the available graphics cards:

```
public enum Graphics: String, CustomStringConvertible {
    case intelUHD617 = "Intel UHD Graphics 617"
    case intelIrisPlus645 = "Intel Iris Plus Graphics 645"
    case radeonProVega20 = "Radeon Pro Vega 20"

    public var description: String {
        self.rawValue
    }
}
```

Whenever a customer selects a configuration, the server assembles a dictionary containing the following keys: "base_model," "size," "processor," and "graphics."

The possible values for base_model are "budget," "office," and "high-end."

In the case of custom configurations, the values for the size, processor, or graphics might be overridden. Possible values for size are "13-inch" and "15-inch". The processor can be "i5," "i7," or "i9" representing Intel Core i5, Intel Core i7, and Intel Core i9.

There are three options for the graphics card: "intel-uhd-graphics-617," "intel-iris-plus-graphics-645" and "radeon-pro-vega-20."

Here's a configuration fetched from the server:

```
{
    "base_model": "budget"
}
```

The customer selected the budget model without further customizations.

In the second setup, the client selected the budget model but decided to upgrade its size from 13-inch to 15-inch.

```
{
    "base_model": "office",
    "size": "15-inch"
}
```

This third configuration contains a Budget model, with upgraded size, processor, and graphics.

```
{
    "base_model": "budget",
    "size": "15-inch",
    "processor": "i7",
    "graphics": "radeon-pro-vega-20"
}
```

Next, we'll try to implement a solution that creates the corresponding laptops based on the configurations fetched from the server.

5.3 Highlighting the Problem

We receive the payload with the configuration values from the server. The next step is to interpret these keys and values. Then, we must create a matching `Laptop` instance.

We need a function that takes the dictionary with the configuration values and returns a `Laptop` instance. Let's call it `buildLaptop()`. It takes a parameter of dictionary type, with keys and values of type `String`.

The configuration we receive from the server may be invalid. Therefore, I make the return type optional.

```
func buildLaptop(configuration: [String: String]) -> Laptop? {
```

Next, I check if the configuration contains a value for the "base_model" key. This value is mandatory. If it's missing, we return nil and exit the function:

```
    guard let model = configuration["base_model"] else {
        return nil
    }
```

I create a variable for the `Laptop` instance. It's optional because we don't yet know if the configuration values are valid.

```
    var laptop: Laptop?
```

I use the switch statement to compare the model against the predefined values.

```
    switch model {
```

If the model is "Budget," I create a laptop instance using 13-inch for size, Intel Core i5 for the processor, and a basic graphics card:

```
    case "budget":
        laptop = Laptop(size: Size.thirteenInch, processor: Pro-
cessor.i5, graphics: Graphics.intelUHD617)
```

The "Office" model should be 15-inch, with an Intel Core i7 processor and Intel Iris Plus 645 graphics card:

```
    case "office":
        laptop = Laptop(size: Size.fifteenInch, processor: Proces-
sor.i7, graphics: Graphics.intelIrisPlus645)
```

The high-end model is the most powerful:

```
    case "high-end":
```

```
    laptop = Laptop(size: Size.fifteenInch, processor: Proces-
sor.i9, graphics: Graphics.radeonProVega20)
```

If the model doesn't match any of these values, I print a warning message.

```
default:
    print("Unexpected value.")
    return nil
}
```

If the laptop instance could not be instantiated, I return nil.

```
guard let selectedLaptop = laptop else {
    return nil
}
```

Otherwise, we go on with parsing the custom settings.

First, we check if there's a custom size—that is, if the dictionary contains a value for the size key.

```
if let customSize = configuration["size"] {
    switch customSize {
```

If it's 13-inch, we update the laptop's size property.

```
case "13-inch":
    selectedLaptop.size = Size.thirteenInch
```

Let's do the same for the 15-inch value:

```
case "15-inch":
    selectedLaptop.size = Size.fifteenInch
```

And I print a warning if there's an unexpected value for the "size" key.

```
default:
    print("Invalid value")
    }
}
```

Next, we retrieve the processor. If the customer decided to change the CPU type, it should be one of the three values, and we set the laptop's processor property accordingly.

This value might also be invalid, so let's print a warning.

```
if let customProcessor = configuration["processor"] {
    switch customProcessor {
    case "i5":
```

```
            selectedLaptop.processor = Processor.i5
        case "i7":
            selectedLaptop.processor = Processor.i7
        case "i9":
            selectedLaptop.processor = Processor.i9
        default:
            print("Invalid value")
        }
    }
```

The user might have customized the graphics card, too. If the graphics card was updated, we check if we received a valid value from the server and update the laptop's graphics property.

```
    if let customGraphics = configuration["graphics"] {
        switch customGraphics {
        case "intel-uhd-graphics-617":
            selectedLaptop.graphics = Graphics.intelUHD617
        case "intel-iris-plus-graphics-645":
            selectedLaptop.graphics = Graphics.intelIrisPlus645
        case "radeon-pro-vega-20":
            selectedLaptop.graphics = Graphics.radeonProVega20
        default:
            print("Invalid value")
        }
    }
```

Finally, we return the configured laptop.

```
    return selectedLaptop
}
```

Now, let's test the function. First, we parse a simple configuration; that should produce a budget laptop:

```
// Create a budget laptop
if let laptop = buildLaptop(configuration: ["base_model": "bud-
get"]) {
    print(laptop)
}
```

The output shows that our function works as expected:

```
13-inch laptop
        Processor Intel Core i5
        Graphics Intel UHD Graphics 617
```

Next, let's try to create an Office laptop. The customer decided to change the size from 15-inch to 13-inch:

```
// A smaller office laptop
if let laptop = buildLaptop(configuration: ["base_model": "office",
                                            "size": "13-inch"]
) {
    print(laptop)
}
```

This passed the test, too:

```
13-inch laptop
        Processor Intel Core i7
        Graphics Intel Iris Plus Graphics 645
```

Last, I parse a configuration that should create a High-End laptop with downgraded size and graphics:

```
// High-End with downgraded size and graphics
if let laptop = buildLaptop(configuration: ["base_model": "high-
end",
                    "size": "13-inch",
                    "graphics": "intel-iris-plus-graphics-645"]) {
    print(laptop)
}
```

This works, too:

```
13-inch laptop
        Processor Intel Core i9
        Graphics Intel Iris Plus Graphics 645
```

We've implemented a working solution that creates and configures laptops based on the configurations received from the server.

The issue with this code is that we delegate a lot of responsibilities to the client. Besides parsing, callers need to know about all the possible configuration values.

Here's where the Builder can help. We're going to refactor our solution next.

5.4 Refactoring Using the Builder

The solution we just implemented works, but the client takes on too many responsibilities and needs to know a lot about the objects it creates.

To alleviate the situation, we're going to refactor our code using the Builder design pattern.

I create a new playground page called LaptopShopWithBuilder. I add a new swift file and copy over the code of our `Laptop` class.

Now, let's add another file called Builder. We start by defining a common protocol that should be adopted by all concrete builders.

```
public protocol LaptopBuilder {
    var size: Size {get set}
    var processor: Processor {get set}
    var graphics: Graphics {get set}

    mutating func buildParts(configuration: [String: String])
    func getLaptop() -> Laptop
}
```

The protocol defines three calculated properties: size, processor, and graphics. It also defines two methods: `buildParts()` and `getLaptop()`. I mark the `buildParts()` method using the mutating keyword, because it changes the internal state of the builder.

Let's revisit the UML diagram of the Builder pattern to understand the purpose of these methods.

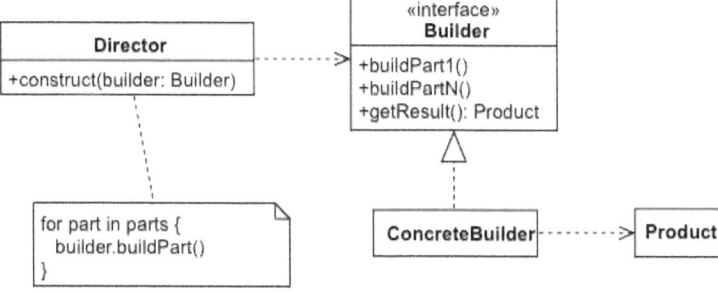

So, `buildParts()` gets invoked by the director to construct the parts of the product. `getLaptop()` returns the finished product.

The logic required to set up a `Laptop` is the same for all builders. Thus, I provide a default implementation in the protocol extension.

We can borrow the code from the `buildLaptop()` function. So, let's switch to the previously implemented playground page and copy the part that parses the customized settings. We need to make some adjustments to make this code compile.

```
extension LaptopBuilder {
    mutating public func buildParts(configuration: [String:
String]) {
        if let customSize = configuration["size"] {
            switch customSize {
            case "13-inch":
                size = Size.thirteenInch
            case "15-inch":
                size = Size.fifteenInch
            default:
                print("Invalid value")
            }
        }

        if let customProcessor = configuration["processor"] {
            switch customProcessor {
            case "i5":
                processor = Processor.i5
            case "i7":
                processor = Processor.i7
            case "i9":
                processor = Processor.i9
            default:
                print("Invalid value")
            }
        }

        if let customGraphics = configuration["graphics"] {
            switch customGraphics {
            case "intel-uhd-graphics-617":
                graphics = Graphics.intelUHD617
            case "intel-iris-plus-graphics-645":
                graphics = Graphics.intelIrisPlus645
            case "radeon-pro-vega-20":
                graphics = Graphics.radeonProVega20
            default:
                print("Invalid value")
            }
        }
    }
}
```

Now, let's also implement the `getLaptop()` method, which returns a `Laptop` object instantiated with the values of the size, processor, and graphics properties:

```
    public func getLaptop() -> Laptop {
        Laptop(size: size,
            processor: processor,
            graphics: graphics)
    }
}
```

Next, I define three concrete builder classes.

We already implemented the methods defined in the protocol. The `Builder` classes will only override the properties to match the specific configurations.

For the `BudgetLaptopBuilder`, I set the size to 13-inch, the processor to Intel Core i5, and the graphics to the basic graphics card.

We also need to make the initializer public.

```
public class BudgetLaptopBuilder: LaptopBuilder {
    public var size = Size.thirteenInch
    public var processor = Processor.i5
    public var graphics = Graphics.intelUHD617
    public init() {}
}
```

Similarly, I define the `OfficeLaptopBuilder` and override the three properties.

```
public class OfficeLaptopBuilder: LaptopBuilder {
    public var size = Size.fifteenInch
    public var processor = Processor.i7
    public var graphics = Graphics.intelIrisPlus645
    public init() {}
}
```

And we need a third builder that encapsulates the defaults for the high-end laptop.

```
public class HighEndLaptopBuilder: LaptopBuilder {
    public var size = Size.fifteenInch
    public var processor = Processor.i9
    public var graphics = Graphics.radeonProVega20
    public init() {}
}
```

We also need a `Director`. It defines an initializer that takes a `Builder` argument. Note that I provide the protocol here so that callers can pass in any of the concrete types. Also, I add a private `builder` property, that gets initialized in the initializer.

```
public class Director {
    private var builder: LaptopBuilder?

    public init(builder: LaptopBuilder?) {
        self.builder = builder
    }
```

The constructLaptop() method relies on the builder to parse the configuration and create the parts.

```
    public func constructLaptop(configuration: [String: String]) {
        builder?.buildParts(configuration: configuration)
    }
}
```

5.5 Using the Revamped Version

Now it's time to switch to the main Playground page.

For each model, we need to instantiate the right builder. I define a function called `createBuilder()`. This function will be responsible to create the right builder based on the configuration.

It takes as input the configuration and returns an object of a type that conforms to the `LaptopBuilder` protocol.

```
func createBuilder(configuration: [String: String]) -> LaptopBuild-
er? {
```

I retrieve the model; if there's no value for this key, I return nil.

```
    guard let model = configuration["base_model"] else {
        return nil
    }
```

Otherwise, we compare the values and return the appropriate builder.

```
    var laptopBuilder: LaptopBuilder?
    switch model {
    case "budget":
        laptopBuilder = BudgetLaptopBuilder()
    case "office":
        laptopBuilder = OfficeLaptopBuilder()
    case "high-end":
        laptopBuilder = HighEndLaptopBuilder()
    default:
        print("Unexpected value.")
    }

    return builder
}
```

That's the only parsing we need to do on the caller side.

Now, we can use the builder as described in the sequence diagram at the beginning of this chapter--that is, we create a `builder`, then instantiate a `director` by passing in the reference to the `builder`:

```
var configuration = ["base_model": "budget"]
var laptopBuilder = createBuilder(configuration: configuration)
var director = Director(builder: laptopBuilder)
```

We invoke the director's `constructLaptop()` method and pass in the configuration. Finally, we retrieve the object by calling the builder's `getLaptop()` method.

```
director.constructLaptop(configuration: configuration)

if let laptop = laptopBuilder?.getLaptop() {
    print(laptop)
}
```

We follow the same sequence for each configuration:

```
configuration = ["base_model": "office",
                 "size": "13-inch"]
laptopBuilder = createBuilder(configuration: configuration)
director = Director(builder: laptopBuilder)
director.constructLaptop(configuration: configuration)

if let laptop = laptopBuilder?.getLaptop() {
    print(laptop)
}

configuration = ["base_model": "high-end",
                 "size": "13-inch",
                 "graphics": "intel-iris-plus-graphics-645"]

laptopBuilder = createBuilder(configuration: configuration)
director = Director(builder: laptopBuilder)
director.constructLaptop(configuration: configuration)

if let laptop = laptopBuilder?.getLaptop() {
    print(laptop)
}
```

The result is the same as without the Builder. However, we got rid of most of the parsing logic from the client. Plus, the caller doesn't need to know about the object's configuration values either.

5.6 Conclusion

The Builder separates the creation of objects from their configuration. It simplifies the creation of instances that need many default values, and when those values don't frequently change when creating new objects.

Don't use the Builder pattern when creating objects that require only a few configuration values, or when those values must change whenever a new instance gets created.

The Builder is similar in purpose to the Factory Method design pattern: both incorporate the creation logic. The key difference between them is that the Builder is useful when building objects that require a complicated setup process.

We'll look into the Factory Method design pattern next.

6. THE FACTORY METHOD

6.1 Overview

Purpose

The Factory Method design pattern is a creational pattern that promotes loose coupling. This pattern lets callers create instances of types that have a common superclass or conform to a given protocol.

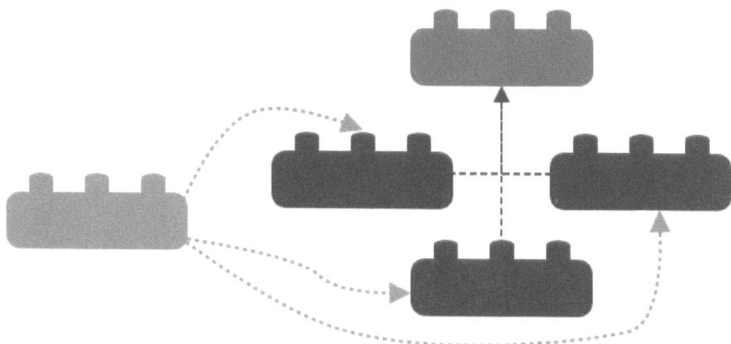

The callers don't need to know the concrete implementation types, just the protocol or the base class.

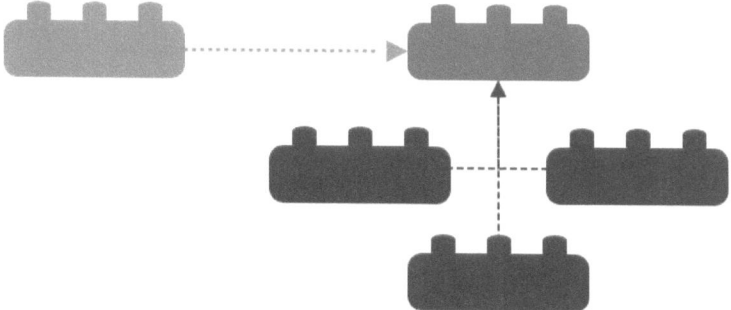

The factory method incorporates the logic required to decide which implementation class to instantiate based on the criteria supplied by the caller. This allows us to eliminate the dependencies between the implementation types and the clients.

Besides reducing the tight coupling in the system, the Factory Method pattern provides further benefits. The exact type is not known; only the methods and calculated properties declared in the protocol are exposed. The other details remain hidden. Thus, we can perform changes without having to refactor the depending components. We can even replace the concrete implementation types or add new ones without affecting the other parts of the system.

Limitations

The Factory Method doesn't have any drawbacks, but its usage is limited to types that share a common protocol or superclass.

Now, you can make those types adopt a protocol or superclass to make them work but only do that if the types are indeed related. You must not enforce protocol conformance to types that have different responsibilities just for the sake of the factory method design pattern.

6.2 The Problem Solved by the Factory Method

To illustrate the problem that is solved by the Factory Method design pattern, we're going to create a protocol and a couple of conforming classes.

Open Xcode and create a playground project called Themes.

We start by defining the `Theme` protocol. It declares two read-only properties, `backgroundColor` and `textColor`, both of type `UIColor`.

```
import UIKit

protocol Theme {
    var backgroundColor: UIColor { get }
    var textColor: UIColor { get }
}
```

Next, we'll implement a few conforming types that provide different background and text color values when callers read their corresponding properties.

The `LightTheme` struct returns white for the background color and black for the text color:

```
struct LightTheme: Theme {
    var backgroundColor = UIColor.white
    var textColor = UIColor.black
}
```

`DarkTheme` returns a black background and white text color:

```
struct DarkTheme: Theme {
    var backgroundColor = UIColor.black
    var textColor = UIColor.white
}
```

Create a `UILabel` instance and apply the colors of the `LightTheme` scheme to it.

```
let label = UILabel(frame: CGRect(x: 0, y: 0, width: 120, height: 44))
label.text = "Hello Swift"

let lightTheme = LightTheme()
label.backgroundColor = lightTheme.backgroundColor
label.textColor = lightTheme.textColor
```

Then we create the `DarkTheme` instance and use its colors to change the label's background and text color:

```
let darkTheme = DarkTheme()
label.backgroundColor = darkTheme.backgroundColor
label.textColor = darkTheme.textColor
```

How about creating a third palette? BrownTheme defines a brown background color and a white text.

```
struct BrownTheme: Theme {
    var backgroundColor = UIColor.brown
    var textColor = UIColor.white
}
```

Again, to apply it, we have to create an instance of the BrownTheme structure.

```
let brownTheme = BrownTheme()
label.backgroundColor = brownTheme.backgroundColor
label.textColor = brownTheme.textColor
```

We have three themes, and we used each of them to decorate the UILabel instance. Although this approach works, it's far from perfect.

The main problem is that clients must know each implementation type to instantiate it directly. In addition, if any of these types changes, or whenever a new theme gets created, the caller code must be adapted. Refactoring a complex code base can be time-consuming and expensive.

Wouldn't it be better if the caller component only knew the protocol and not the implementation classes themselves?

We're going to address these issues in the next section.

6.3 Embedding the Factory Method in the Base Class

Instead of exposing all the concrete theme types, clients should only know the Theme protocol.

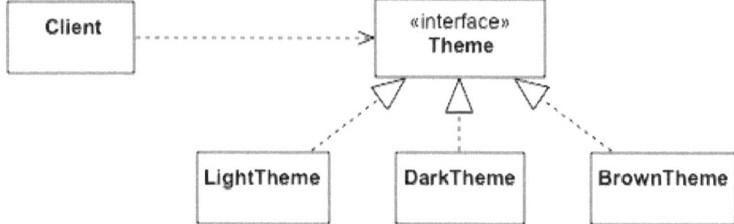

At the core of the Factory Method pattern is a method that encapsulates object creation. The method takes an argument that identifies the implementation class. This argument is usually an enumeration or a predefined constant.

Let's create an enumeration called Themes with three cases that match our types:

```
enum Themes {
    case light
    case dark
    case brown
}
```

Now we can start defining a function responsible for creating the Theme objects. Let's call it makeTheme(_:). The function's parameter would be of type Themes—the enumeration that identifies the types:

```
func makeTheme(_ type: Themes) -> Theme {}
```

The method's return type should be the common protocol or the base class instead of a concrete type. In our case, the return type is the Theme protocol:

```
func makeTheme(_ type: Themes) -> Theme {
    let result: Theme
    switch type {
        case .light: result = LightTheme()
        case .dark: result = DarkTheme()
        case .brown: result = BrownTheme()
    }
    return result
}
```

The function checks the input argument and returns the corresponding Theme instance. Callers only know the protocol and the enumeration that defines the possible `Theme` types. The real implementation types—`LightTheme`, `DarkTheme`, and `BrownTheme`—are not exposed to the callers.

If we need a `DarkTheme` instance, we call the `makeTheme(_:)` function and pass in the value `Themes.dark`

```
let darkTheme = makeTheme(Themes.dark)
```

The returned object is of type `DarkTheme`, but that's hidden from the caller. All he knows is that he received an object of a type that conforms to the `Theme` protocol, and that object has two read-only properties.

```
label.backgroundColor = darkTheme.backgroundColor
label.textColor = darkTheme.textColor
```

Similarly, we can create a `BrownTheme` instance and access its properties:

```
let brownTheme = makeTheme(Themes.brown)
label.backgroundColor = brownTheme.backgroundColor
label.textColor = brownTheme.textColor
```

If you prefer to avoid global functions, you can embed the `makeTheme(_:)` method in a dedicated factory type.

```
struct ThemeFactory {
    static func makeTheme(_ type: Themes) -> Theme {
        let result: Theme
        switch type {
            case .light: result = LightTheme()
            case .dark: result = DarkTheme()
            case .brown: result = BrownTheme()
        }
        return result
    }
}
```

We can now use the new `ThemeFactory`'s `makeTheme(_:)` method without polluting the global namespace:

```
let lightTheme = ThemeFactory.makeTheme(Themes.light)
```

The Factory Method is one of the most straightforward and frequently used creational design patterns. By hiding the details, changes in the implementation types won't have ripple effects on the caller side.

6.4 Conclusion

The Factory Method pattern is a good choice if we want to prevent exposing all the implementation types to our callers. Callers need only know about the protocol or the base class, which reduces the dependencies within the system.

This pattern allows changing the existing implementation types or adding new ones without exposing their details to the components that rely on them.

Note that the Factory Method design pattern cannot be applied when there is no common protocol or shared base class.

7. THE ABSTRACT FACTORY

7.1 Overview

Purpose

The purpose of the Abstract Factory is to provide an abstraction for creating families of related or dependent objects. The calling component doesn't know the concrete types involved in the creation process. Callers should only interact with protocols or base classes to instantiate and use the families of objects.

The following class diagram provides an overview of the Abstract Factory design pattern:

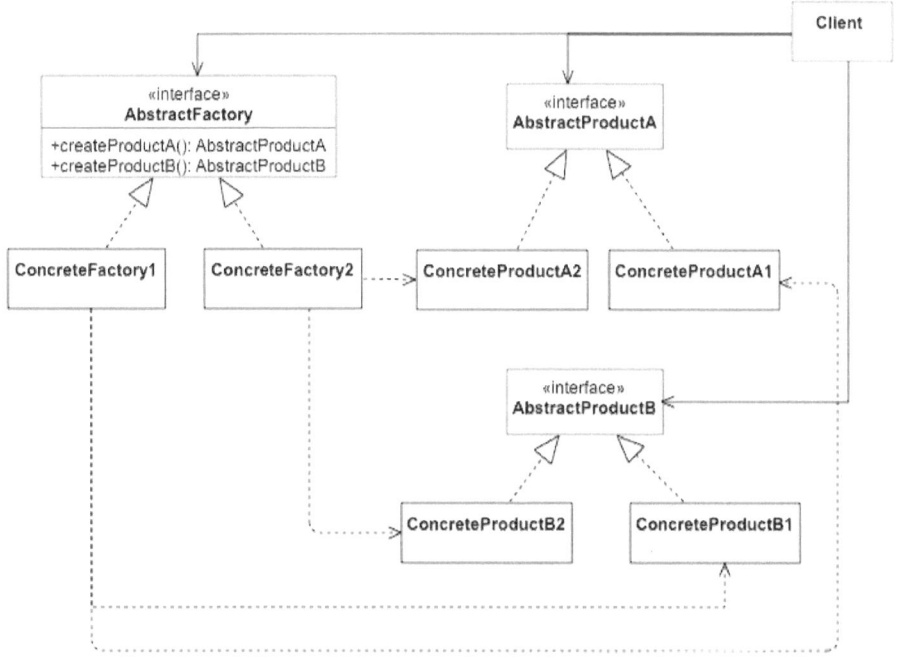

The AbstractFactory defines the operations that create abstract products. The ConcreteFactory types implement the interface declared by the AbstractFactory. We have an abstract product for each family of products. The concrete products implement the abstract product interfaces. In Swift, the abstract factory and the abstract product types would be protocols or base classes.

The following UML diagram depicts a real-world example of the Abstract Factory.

The client deals exclusively with the ComputerFactory and the three abstract products. The calling component doesn't interact with the concrete factories or any of the products directly. Thus, we can change these implementation types without affecting the components that use them.

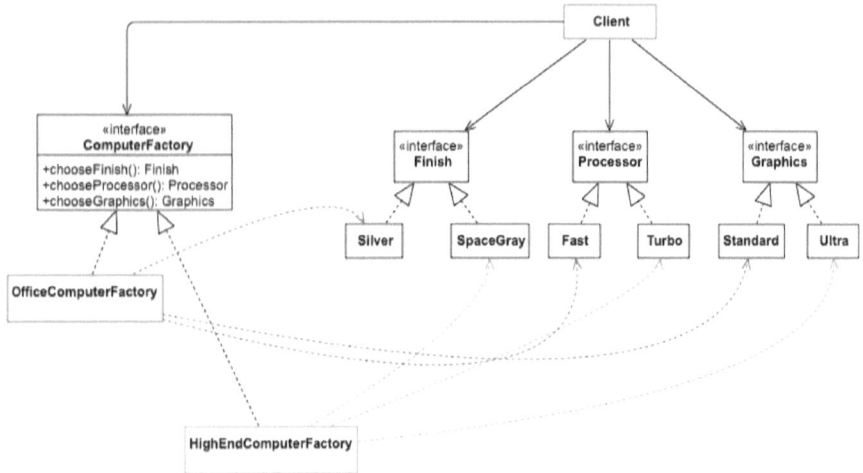

We can create various product configurations by simply changing the concrete factory. The computer assembled by the OfficeComputerFactory will be different from the one built by the HighEndComputerFactory.

This pattern is similar to the Factory Method, but you should use the Abstract Factory to obtain a set of related objects instead of just one.

At this point, I think we've covered enough ground to start working with a real-world example.

7.2 The Problem We Want to Solve

I've gone ahead and implemented a Playground project called ComputerShop.

The Configurations.swift file contains the protocols and concrete types that represent the parts used to configure a computer. To keep it simple, I only defined three protocols and a couple of concrete types for each.

```swift
public protocol Finish: CustomStringConvertible {
    var color: String {get}
    var price: Int {get}
}

extension Finish {
    public var description: String {
        "\(color)"
    }
}
```

The Finish protocol has two properties: color and price.

```swift
public struct Silver: Finish {
    public let color = "silver"
    public let price = 200
    public init() {}
}

public struct SpaceGray: Finish {
    public let color = "space gray"
    public let price = 300
    public init() {}
}
```

The Silver and the SpaceGray structures conform to this protocol and define the corresponding colors. The SpaceGray finish is a bit more expensive than the Silver one.

The next protocol represents the Processor, and it defines a type and a price property.

```swift
public protocol Processor: CustomStringConvertible {
    var type: String {get}
    var price: Int {get}
}

extension Processor {
    public var description: String {
```

```
        "\(type)"
    }
}
```

There are two conforming structures: `Fast` and `Turbo`.

```
public struct Fast: Processor {
    public let type = "fast"
    public let price = 300
    public init() {}
}

public struct Turbo: Processor {
    public let type = "turbo"
    public let price = 500
    public init() {}
}
```

Finally, the `Graphics` protocol defines the card and the `price` property. The concrete types that implement this interface are the `Standard` and the `Ultra` structures.

```
public protocol Graphics: CustomStringConvertible {
    var card: String {get}
    var price: Int {get}
}

extension Graphics {
    public var description: String {
        "\(card)"
    }
}

public struct Standard: Graphics {
    public let card = "standard"
    public let price = 400
    public init() {}
}

public struct Ultra: Graphics {
    public let card = "ultra"
    public let price = 600
    public init() {}
}
```

The client can create different computer configurations using these parts. Let's define a `Computer` type first. I declare it as a structure.

```
struct Computer: {
```

Next, I add the finish, the processor, and the graphics properties:

```
var finish: Finish
var processor: Processor
var graphics: Graphics
```

Let's also add a `price` property. I make this a computed property, and it should return the total price of the given configuration.

```
var price: Int {
    return finish.price + processor.price + graphics.price
}
```

As usual, I'll add a custom description by making this type adopt the `CustomStringConvertible` protocol:

```
struct Computer: CustomStringConvertible {
```

And here's the custom description:

```
var description: String {
    "\nYour configuration: \n\tFinish: \(finish)\n\tProcessor: \
(processor) \n\tGraphics: \(graphics)\n\t$\(price)"
}
```

The next step is to try out what we've implemented so far. Let's create two computers. The first one, called `officeComputer`, gets created using the cheaper parts:

```
let officeComputer = Computer(finish: Silver(), processor: Fast(),
graphics: Standard())
print(officeComputer)
```

The `highEndComputer` has the more expensive parts:

```
let highEndComputer = Computer(finish: SpaceGray(), processor: Tur-
bo(), graphics: Ultra())
print(highEndComputer)
```

Execute the playground. It produces the following console output:

```
Your configuration:
        Finish: silver
        Processor: fast
        Graphics: standard
        $900
```

```
Your configuration:
      Finish: space gray
      Processor: turbo
      Graphics: ultra
      $1400
```

The situation is similar to the one we solved with the Factory Method in the previous chapter: we expose the implementation classes to the callers. This is another classic example of tight coupling, which we should avoid.

The Abstract Factory can save the day. Let's see how.

7.3 Applying the Abstract Factory

We're going to revamp our ComputerShop demo using the Abstract Factory.

I start by creating a new playground page called "ComputerShopWithAbstractFactory." Next, I add a new file which will include the Abstract Factory related types and definitions.

I begin my code by defining the abstract factory.

The three methods define the interface that needs to be implemented by the concrete factory types. The default implementation returns nil.

```
public class ComputerFactory {
    public func chooseFinish() -> Finish? {
        return nil
    }
    override func chooseProcessor() -> Processor? {
        return Fast()
    }
    override func chooseGraphics() -> Graphics? {
        return Standard()
    }
}
```

We could've defined the ComputerFactory as a protocol. I decided to make it a class because I'm about to add a nice feature. We'll expose a factory method that lets clients create a concrete factory without knowing its implementation type.

The makeFactory() method takes a parameter that identifies the kind of factory to create. The return type is the base class, that is, the ComputerFactory.

```
    public final class func makeFactory(type: ComputerType) -> Com-
puterFactory {
```

The ComputerType enumeration has two cases: office and highEnd. We'll return a dedicated factory for each.

```
public enum ComputerType {
    case office
    case highEnd
}
```

The makeFactory() method checks the input argument and creates the corresponding factory.

```
    public final class func makeFactory(type: ComputerType)
-> ComputerFactory {
        var factory: ComputerFactory

        switch(type) {
        case .office: factory = OfficeComputerFactory()
        case .highEnd: factory = HighEndComputerFactory()
        }

        return factory
    }
```

Next, we need to define the two factories themselves. OfficeComputerFactory inherits from the ComputerFactory class, and it overrides its methods. The implementation is straightforward: we return Silver for finish, Fast for processor, and Standard for the graphics.

```
private class OfficeComputerFactory: ComputerFactory {
    override func chooseFinish() -> Finish? {
        return Silver()
    }
    override func chooseProcessor() -> Processor? {
        return Fast()
    }
    override func chooseGraphics() -> Graphics? {
        return Standard()
    }
}
```

HighEndComputerFactory returns the more expensive parts:

```
private class HighEndComputerFactory: ComputerFactory {
    override func chooseFinish() -> Finish? {
        return SpaceGray()
    }
    override func chooseProcessor() -> Processor? {
        return Turbo()
    }
    override func chooseGraphics() -> Graphics? {
        return Ultra()
    }
}
```

We're ready to use our abstract factory. But before that, I copy over the code from the previous playground.

We can create a factory by calling the ComputerFactory's makeFactory() method.

```
var factory = ComputerFactory.makeFactory(type: ComputerType.of-
fice)
```

Let's define a helper function that takes a factory argument and returns an optional `Computer` instance. This helper prevents us from writing the same code over and over again.

```
func createComputer(factory: ComputerFactory) -> Computer? {
    guard let finish = factory.chooseFinish(),
        let processor = factory.chooseProcessor(),
        let graphics = factory.chooseGraphics() else {
            return nil
    }

    return Computer(finish: finish, processor: processor, graphics:
graphics)
}
```

We invoke the factory methods to create the various parts. If any of these calls fail, we return nil. Otherwise, we return a computer instance.

After all these preparations, we can finally remove the unwanted dependencies.

```
let officeComputer = Computer(finish: Silver(), processor: Fast(),
graphics: Standard())
```

The `createComputer()` function relies on the factory to create the various parts and configure the computer instance. We don't have to provide concrete `Finish`, `Processor`, or `Graphics` objects to the `Computer` initializer.

```
if let officeComputer = createComputer(factory: factory) {
    print(officeComputer)
}
```

To create a high-end configuration, we need the matching factory. So, I'm going to pass in `ComputerType.highEnd` to the factory method.

```
factory = ComputerFactory.makeFactory(type: ComputerType.highEnd)
if let highEndComputer = createComputer(factory: factory) {
    print(highEndComputer)
}
```

That's it! We used the Abstract Factory combined with the Factory Method to create a loosely coupled system.

7.4 Conclusion

The Abstract Factory should be used if we want to create families of related or dependent objects.

This design pattern removes the dependencies between the caller component and the concrete factories and product types. This decoupling makes it possible to modify the factories or the products without affecting the components that use them.

Another benefit is that we can switch between product configurations easily. We can create a different family of objects simply by changing the concrete factory.

Don't use the Abstract Factory to create single objects. In such cases, you should consider using the Factory Method instead.

8. THE ADAPTER

8.1 Overview

Purpose

More often than not, we rely on third-party libraries or frameworks. Consequently, we have to use types that do not fit well into our system. Their public interface is different, and we can't change it since it's not our code.

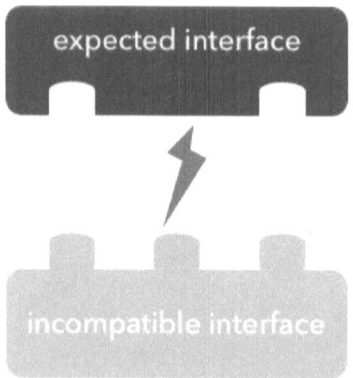

We can't modify the incompatible interface, but refactoring our existing code is not a viable solution either. The Adapter design pattern provides an elegant solution to this problem: it hides the incompatible type and exposes an interface that's familiar to the caller.

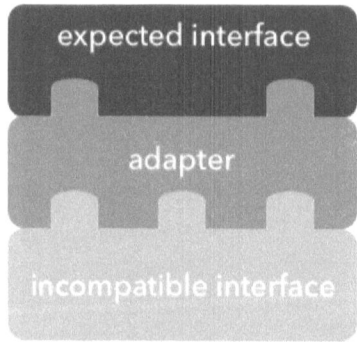

The adapter wraps the object to be adapted and exposes the interface we need. The caller uses the adapter, which in turn converts the calls to ones that make sense to the wrapped type. The adapter returns the results to the caller through the compatible interface.

In addition to the classical approach, Swift lets us implement the Adapter using type extensions. This language feature allows for enhancing any type without touching its implementation. We don't need to introduce a wrapper type.

Instead, we define the new methods and calculated properties in an extension.

This pattern is useful when we need to integrate a component that provides similar functionality to other components in the system but comes with an incompatible interface.

Pitfalls

One common mistake when implementing the Adapter is trying to adapt an interface that doesn't provide the expected functionality. So, make sure that you're using the right component before trying to make it work with the rest of the system.

8.2 Motivation for Using the Adapter

We'll start with an example to demonstrate the benefits of the Adapter pattern.

Create a new playground project called PaymentGateways. I've implemented a family of payment gateway classes that conform to the `PaymentGateway` protocol:

```
protocol PaymentGateway {
    func receivePayment(amount: Double)
    var totalPayments: Double {get}
}
```

The protocol declares the `receivePayment(amount:)` method and a read-only calculated property called `totalPayments`.

The `PayPal` and the `Stripe` classes adopt the `PaymentGateway` protocol. The `receivePayment(amount:)` method adds the input argument's value to the private `total` property. The `totalPayments` calculated property outputs a log message and returns the accumulated total.

```
class PayPal: PaymentGateway {
    private var total = 0.0

    func receivePayment(amount: Double) {
        total += amount
    }

    var totalPayments: Double {
        print("Total payments received via PayPal: \(total)")
        return total
    }
}

class Stripe: PaymentGateway {
    private var total = 0.0

    func receivePayment(amount: Double) {
        total += amount
    }

    var totalPayments: Double {
        print("Total payments received via Venmo: \(total)")
        return total
    }
}
```

We can create a `PayPal` object, and call its `receivePayment(amount:)` method to simulate payments through PayPal:

```
let paypal = PayPal()
paypal.receivePayment(amount: 100)
paypal.receivePayment(amount: 200)
paypal.receivePayment(amount: 499)
```

And if we want to receive payments over Stripe, we just create a `Stripe` instance and invoke the `receivePayment(amount:)` method:

```
let stripe = Stripe()
stripe.receivePayment(amount: 5.99)
stripe.receivePayment(amount: 25)
stripe.receivePayment(amount: 9.99)
```

To calculate the total payments received through all the payment gateways, we can iterate through the list of `Stripe` and `PayPal` objects.

First, create a list called `paymentGateways`. It can hold objects of types that conform to the `PaymentGateway` protocol. Initialize the list with the `paypal` and the `stripe` objects:

```
var paymentGateways: [PaymentGateway] = [paypal, stripe]
```

The total gets calculated in the for-in loop that iterates through all the objects in the `paymentGateways` list. The value of their `totalPayments` property gets added to the running total.

```
var total = 0.0
for gateway in paymentGateways {
    total += gateway.totalPayments
}
```

This code relies on polymorphism. The `paymentGateways` array contains objects that conform to the `PaymentGateway` protocol; this lets us use the methods and the properties declared in the common protocol.

Finally, print the total payments.

```
print(total)
```

Now, let's assume that we have to use a third-party framework to process Amazon payments.

```
// Third-party class that doesn't conform to PaymentGateway
class AmazonPayments {
```

```
    var payments = 0.0

    func paid(value: Double, currency: String) {
        payments += value
        print("Paid \(currency)\(value) via Amazon Payments")
    }

    func fulfilledTransactions() -> Double {
        return payments
    }
}
```

Although the AmazonPayments type provides the functionality we need, its interface is entirely different. The AmazonPayments class does not conform to our PaymentGateway protocol. Thus, we can't easily integrate it with our code.

Let me illustrate the problem. We can create an AmazonPayments instance and then call its paid(value:, currency:) method to receive payments:

```
let amazonPayments = AmazonPayments()
amazonPayments.paid(value: 120, currency: "USD")
amazonPayments.paid(value: 74.99, currency: "USD")
```

However, we can't append the AmazonPayments instance to the list of gateways because the AmazonPayments class doesn't conform to the PaymentGateway protocol:

```
paymentGateways.append(amazonPayments) // this line won't compile
```

Thus, we can't use it in our for-in loop as we did with the paypal and the stripe objects.

```
for gateway in paymentGateways {
    total += gateway.totalPayments
}
```

We can't rely on the elegance of polymorphism since the third-party type doesn't share a common protocol with our other payment gateway classes.

Integrating the incompatible type in our system would require additional lines of code whenever we try to use it. We can avoid the proliferation of such code by employing the Adapter pattern.

8.3 The Object Adapter

We're going to implement a wrapper around the `AmazonPayments` instance. Let's call this wrapper class `AmazonPaymentsAdapter` and make it conform to the `PaymentGateway` protocol:

```
class AmazonPaymentsAdapter: PaymentGateway {}
```

We need to add the `receivePayment(amount: Double)` method and the `totalPayments` property:

```
class AmazonPaymentsAdapter: PaymentGateway {
    func receivePayment(amount: Double) {}
    var totalPayments: Double {}
}
```

The wrapped object should be an `AmazonPayments` instance. So let's add a private property called `amazonPayments` and initialize it:

```
    private let amazonPayments = AmazonPayments()
```

The `receivePayment(amount:)` method delegates the call to the `AmazonPayments paid(value:, currency:)` method. Since `receivePayment(amount:)` does not have a currency parameter, the currency defaults to US dollars:

```
    func receivePayment(amount: Double) {
        amazonPayments.paid(value: amount, currency: "USD")
    }
```

The `totalPayments` property returns the value of the wrapped object's payments property:

```
    var totalPayments: Double {
        let total = amazonPayments.payments
        print("Total payments received via Amazon Payments: \(to-
tal)")
        return total
    }
```

Now, we can create an `AmazonPaymentsAdapter` instance instead of using the `AmazonPayments` type directly:

```
let amazonPaymentsAdapter = AmazonPaymentsAdapter()
amazonPaymentsAdapter.receivePayment(amount: 120)
amazonPaymentsAdapter.receivePayment(amount: 74.99)
```

The adapter conforms to the `PaymentGateway` protocol; thus, we can use it together with the other conforming types:

```
paymentGateways.append(amazonPaymentsAdapter)

var sum = 0.0
for gateway in paymentGateways {
    sum += gateway.totalPayments
}

print(sum)
```

The code looks clean: there's no conditional logic referencing the incompatible `AmazonPayments` type. The caller doesn't even know that we're relying on third-party code. And that's exactly the point of the Adapter design pattern.

8.4 Swift Extensions

Swift extensions provide the ability to extend types even if we don't have access to their source code.

We can add new behavior to existing classes, structures, enumerations or protocols. The concept is similar to Objective-C categories, except that Swift extensions do not have names.

Here's what we can do with extensions:

→ Add computed type and instance properties

→ Define instance and type methods

→ Provide new initializers

→ Define subscripts

→ Create and use new nested types

→ Make existing types conform to a protocol

Let's explore these options through practical examples.

1. Swift extensions let us add computed instance properties and computed type properties.

In this example, we add two new computed type instances to the type Double.

```
extension Double {
    public var celsius: Double { return self }
    public var fahrenheit: Double { return (self * 1.8) + 32 }
}
// Testing
let boilingWater = 100.0
print("Water boils at \(boilingWater)°C / \(boilingWater.fahren-
heit)°F")
```

These new properties express that a `Double` value should be considered as a certain temperature unit. The `Double` value of 1 represents 1 degree Celsius. To convert temperatures from Celsius to Fahrenheit, we have to multiply by 1.8 and add 32.

2. With Swift extensions, we can define instance methods and type methods.

Now, we are going to enhance the `String` type with a method which returns whether the string is lowercase.

```
extension String {
    public func isLowercase() -> Bool {
        return self == self.lowercased()
    }
}

// Testing
let string = "abcdef"
print("String \(string) is lowercase: \(string.isLowercase())")
let string2 = "Abcdef"
print("String \(string2) is lowercase: \(string2.isLowercase())")
```

3. If we want to provide new initializers to existing types without modifying their source, Swift extensions are the way to go.

Let's add an initializer to the `CGVector` structure.

```
extension CGVector {
    public init(point: CGPoint) {
        self.init(dx: point.x, dy: point.y)
    }
}
```

This new `init(point:)` method allows creating a vector from a `CGPoint` value.

```
// Testing
let vec2D = CGVector(point: CGPoint(x: 2, y: 5))
print("CGVector \(vec2D) initialized with CGPoint")
```

4. We can even add subscripts via extensions.

We're going to add an integer subscript to the `String` type.

```
extension String {
    public subscript (index: Int) -> Character {
        guard index >= 0 else {
            return ""
        }

        guard let idx = self.index(self.startIndex, offsetBy: in-
dex, limitedBy: self.endIndex) else {
            return ""
        }
```

```
        return self[idx]
    }
}
```

This subscript returns the character at a given index in the string. For invalid indexes, the subscript returns the "🍎" character.

5. Extensions can also add new nested types to existing classes, enums, and structures.

This snippet adds a new nested enumeration called `CaseType` to `String`.

```
extension String {
    public enum CaseType {
        case lowerCase, upperCase, mixedCase
    }

    public var caseType: CaseType {
        switch self {
        case let str where str == str.uppercased():
            return .upperCase
        case let str where str == str.lowercased():
            return .lowerCase
        default:
            return .mixedCase
        }
    }
}
```

The `CaseType` enumeration shows whether a string contains only lowercase, only uppercase, or mixed-case letters.

```
// Testing
let strLower = "abcdef"
print("\(strLower) is \(strLower.caseType)")
let strMixed = "Abcdef"
print("\(strMixed) is \(strMixed.caseType)")
let strUpper = "ABCDEF"
print("\(strUpper) is \(strUpper.caseType)")
```

6. Last but not least, with Swift extensions we can make existing types conform to a protocol.

I'm going to show you a detailed example in the next section.

8.5 Adapter using Type Extensions

In Swift, we are able to implement the Adapter pattern without creating a new wrapper type.

There is a straightforward and elegant way to add the missing methods to the `AmazonPayments` class through a powerful Swift language feature called extension.

Type extensions are a convenient way to add protocol conformance to a type without modifying its source code.

Let's declare an `AmazonPayments` extension that adopts the `PaymentGateway` protocol:

```
extension AmazonPayments: PaymentGateway {
```

We can copy the `receivePayment(amount:)` method and the `totalPayments` calculated property from the `AmazonPaymentsAdapter` and replace the references to the `amazonPayments` wrapped object to self:

```
    func receivePayment(amount: Double) {
        amazonPaymentsself.paid(value: amount, currency: "USD")
    }

    var totalPayments: Double {
        let total = amazonPaymentsself.payments
        print("Total payments received via Amazon Payments: \(to-
tal)")
        return total
    }
```

And now, we can get rid of the `AmazonPaymentsAdapter`.

```
// Remove the wrapper
class AmazonPaymentsAdapter: PaymentGateway {}
```

We managed to add the `PaymentGateway` protocol conformance through the `AmazonPayments` xtension. Now we can use the new type without issues:

```
let amazonPayments = AmazonPayments()
amazonPayments.receivePayment(amount: 120)
amazonPayments.receivePayment(amount: 74.99)
```

We can append the `AmazonPayments` instance to the `paymentGateways` list and rely on polymorphism to access it:

```
paymentGateways.append(amazonPayments)
var sum = 0.0
for gateway in paymentGateways {
    sum += gateway.totalPayments
}

print(sum)
```

With the type extension approach, there's no need to add a wrapper type. While this is a very intuitive and straightforward way to implement an Adapter, it only works if there is a common protocol.

8.6 Conclusion

The Adapter pattern converts an incompatible interface into one that we need.

This pattern should be used to make things work after they are designed. Use the Adapter if you cannot change the source code of the incompatible type.

Swift extensions let us enhance a type without modifying its implementation. You can also wrap the adapter object in a dedicated Adapter class which exposes the interface that we need.

The Adapter can save us from a lot of refactoring work when integrating third-party or legacy code.

9. THE DECORATOR

9.1 Overview

Purpose

The Decorator design pattern allows adding new behavior to existing types dynamically. We can extend the functionality of a type without modifying its implementation, which is a flexible alternative to subclassing.

The decorator can be implemented by wrapping the object to be enhanced. Another way to extend an existing type is by using Swift type extensions. Extensions provide the ability to add additional methods to types without having to subclass or change their source code.

I am going to show you how to implement the decorator via both object wrapping and Swift extensions.

Pitfalls

One of the common mistakes when implementing the decorator is adding an unrelated behavior to a type. Make sure that you don't violate the Single Responsibility Principle, which tells us that each type should have one, well-defined responsibility.

9.1 UIColor Enhancements through Extensions

In this demo, we are going to enhance the `UIColor` type so that it can create color instances from HTML color codes.

Start Xcode and create a new playground project called UIColorExtension.

We use Swift extensions to add a new `UIColor` initializer which takes a 32-bit unsigned integer as the input argument.

```
extension UIColor {
    convenience init(hex: UInt32) {}
}
```

This argument represents the HTML color code. HTML color codes are provided as hexadecimal triplets representing the colors red, green, and blue in the form #RRGGBB. Here are a few examples:

→ 0xFF0000 represents the color red

→ 0x00FF00 is the color green

→ 0x0000FF is blue

The `UIColor` initializer expects float values in the range [0..1]. Therefore, we need to extract the byte values from the HTML color code, and convert the red, green, and blue components from byte values in the range [0..255] to floating point values.

The red component is obtained by performing a bitwise AND between the input value and the hexadecimal value 0xFF0000. The zeros in the 0xFF0000 will mask the second and third bytes of the input integer.

After shifting the result 16 places to the right and dividing it by 255, we get the red component as float value in the range 0..1:

```
    convenience init(hex: UInt32) {
        let divisor = CGFloat(255)
        let red     = CGFloat((hex & 0xFF0000) >> 16) / divisor
```

We use similar logic to calculate the green and the blue values, except that the masks are different.

```
        let green   = CGFloat((hex & 0x00FF00) >> 8) / divisor
        let blue    = CGFloat(hex & 0x0000FF) / divisor
```

For the blue value, we don't need to shift the result since the blue component is represented by the lowest byte.

Now we can call the `self.init(red:, green:, blue:, alpha:)` method with the converted red, green, and blue values.

```
self.init(red: red, green: green, blue: blue, alpha: 1)
```

We can now create a `UIColor` instances from HTML color codes:

```
let darkBlue = UIColor(hex: 0x191970)
let lightBlue = UIColor(hex: 0x3CB5B5)
let customYellow = UIColor(hex: 0xFCD920)

let customRed = UIColor(hex: 0xE53B51)
```

When we run the demo, the colors are generated using the new initializer. We just enhanced the `UIColor` class through an extension.

Without extensions, we would need to subclass or wrap the `UIColor` class; however, introducing a new type does not provide the same seamless experience as using an already existing, well-known type.

Moreover, the new functionality we provide in a type extension is available on all existing instances of that type, including those created before defining the extension.

9.2 Overriding Stored Properties

Extensions can be used to add new behavior to existing types without modifying their code. There is one exception, though: we cannot add or override stored properties.

To add new stored properties to a type, we can create a subclass or we can decorate the original object.

Decorators can modify the behavior of an object at runtime, which is not possible via subclassing. By decorating an object, you won't affect the other objects of the same type. The Decorator implements the same interface as the component it is going to decorate.

Decorators can modify the existing behavior or add new functionality to a type. The decorator stores an instance of the wrapped component and forwards requests to this object. The original behavior can be modified by making changes before or after calling the method of the wrapped component.

We are going to implement a `UILabel` decorator which allows creating rounded labels with custom borders. The `BorderedLabelDecorator` is a subclass of `UILabel` and wraps a `UILabel` instance.

```
class BorderedLabelDecorator: UILabel {
    fileprivate let wrappedLabel: UILabel

}
```

The label instance is stored in the wrappedLabel private property. Callers pass the `UILabel` object in the initializer method, along with some other arguments required to decorate the label. Let's provide some defaults for the `cornerRadius`, `borderWidth`, and `borderColor`.

```
    required init(label: UILabel, cornerRadius: CGFloat = 3.0,
borderWidth: CGFloat = 1.0, borderColor: UIColor = .black) {
```

Whenever we set a property of the `BorderedLabelDecorator`, the value gets assigned to the wrappedLabel instance.

```
        self.wrappedLabel = label
```

Note that we must call super `init(frame:)` with a valid frame to initialize the superclass in order to set up the properties:

95

```
            super.init(frame: label.frame)
            wrappedLabel.layer.cornerRadius = cornerRadius
            wrappedLabel.layer.borderColor = borderColor.cgColor
            wrappedLabel.layer.borderWidth = borderWidth
            wrappedLabel.clipsToBounds = true
    }
```

Next, we override the properties we are interested in, namely: `textAlignment`, `backgroundColor`, `textColor`, and `text`.

For the `textAlignment`, `backgroundColor`, and `textColor` properties we just forward the requests to the `wrappedLabel` instance:

```
    override var textAlignment: NSTextAlignment {
        get {
            return wrappedLabel.textAlignment
        }
        set {
            wrappedLabel.textAlignment = newValue
        }
    }

    override var backgroundColor: UIColor? {
        get {
            return wrappedLabel.backgroundColor
        }
        set {
            wrappedLabel.backgroundColor = newValue
        }
    }

    override var textColor: UIColor? {
        get {
            return wrappedLabel.textColor
        }
        set {
            wrappedLabel.textColor = newValue
        }
    }
```

However, we use a different approach for the `text` property: when a new value is set, we add a funny character at the beginning and at the end of the input string:

```
    override var text: String? {
        get {
            return wrappedLabel.text
```

```
        }
        set {
            var str = "*"
            if let newVal = newValue {
                str += newVal + str
            }
            wrappedLabel.text = str
        }
    }
}
```

We must also override the layer property to make sure that we return the layer of the wrapped `UILabel` instance.

```
override var layer: CALayer {
    return wrappedLabel.layer
}
```

Now we can create a `UILabel` instance and decorate it so that it appears with rounded corners and modified text.

```
var roundedLabel = BorderedLabelDecorator(label: label, cornerRa-
dius: 10, borderWidth: 1, borderColor: .red)
roundedLabel.textAlignment = .center
roundedLabel.backgroundColor = .white
roundedLabel.textColor = lightBlue

roundedLabel.text = "Rounded label with border and custom text"
```

Note that we can use any `BorderedLabelDecorator` object as a substitute for `UILabel` instances.

9.3 Conclusion

The Decorator design pattern allows changing the behavior of objects. The functionality of existing types can be extended without subclassing or modifying their source code.

Wrapping the object to be enhanced is one way to implement the Decorator. Another option is to use Swift extensions.

We cannot add new stored properties with extensions. If you have to add a new property, consider making it a computed property. If this is not an option, you'll need to either subclass the original type or use object wrapping.

As a last hint: avoid changing the original purpose of a type by decorating it with unrelated behavior.

10. THE FACADE

10.1 Overview

Purpose

The Façade wraps one or more components to simplify their usage. It hides the complexity and lets us work with a more convenient interface.

The Façade pattern consolidates the functionality into a single class and hides the complexity by providing a simpler interface. Clients don't have to use the complicated subsystem directly. Instead, they communicate with the façade which in turn forwards the requests to the components it simplifies.

The Façade not only simplifies the usage of complex interfaces, but it also decouples the consumer side from these complicated frameworks.

You may want to use the Façade when you only need a subset of the functionality provided by a type or framework. It also proves to be useful also when working with components that tend to change frequently; SDKs and frameworks that are still under development are perfect candidates for the Façade. Changes in these frameworks can be adopted in the Façade, without having to refactor the client code. This separation can be a huge time saver.

Cons of the Façade

The Façade pattern is simple and easy to implement. You should avoid adding too many responsibilities to your façade. Another pitfall is exposing the types it simplifies. The consumer should only interact with the façade and not the underlying types. Otherwise, we lose the benefits of this pattern.

10.2 Exposing NLP Features through a Façade

In the following demo, we're going to build a Façade class that provides a simplified interface to work with the NaturalLanguage framework.

We start with a playground project called NLPFacadeDemo.

First, add a new Swift file called NLPFacade.swift. Next, import the NaturalLanguage framework:

```
import NaturalLanguage
```

Now, let's create a public class called NLPFacade.

```
public class NLPFacade {
```

This class will expose a couple of public methods. The first method will return the dominant language of the input text.

```
    public class func dominantLanguage(for string: String) ->
String? {
```

The method analyzes the input text and returns the language or nil if it can't recognize the language.

To identify the language, we rely on the NLLanguageRecognizer class. Its dominantLanguage(for:) type method takes text as input and returns an optional NLLanguage instance:

```
    public class func dominantLanguage(for string: String) ->
String? {
        let language = NLLanguageRecognizer.dominantLanguage(for:
string)
        return language?.rawValue
    }
```

The next public method will identify the parts of speech in a string.

```
    public class func partsOfSpeech(for text: String) -> [WordLex-
icalClassPair] {
```

The method's parameter is the string we're going to analyze, and the return type is an array of word - lexical class pairs. We need to define the WordLexicalClassPair structure first. Insert the following structure right above the NLPFacade declaration:

```
public struct WordLexicalClassPair {
```

```
    let word: String
    let lexicalClass: String
}
```

`WordLexicalClassPair` has two properties: `word` and `lexicalClass`, both of type `String`. I also add a custom description by adopting the `CustomStringConvertible` protocol:

```
public struct WordLexicalClassPair: CustomStringConvertible {
    let word: String
    let lexicalClass: String

    public var description: String {
        return "\"\(word)\": \(lexicalClass)"
    }
}
```

And now, we can implement the `partsOfSpeech(for text: String)` method. But first, we need a natural language tagger instance.

`NLTagger` supports different languages. We can use it to segment text into words, sentences, or paragraphs. It can also identify the lexical class or other properties of the detected units.

Create a private static property called `tagger`. The `NLTagger` initializer takes a list of tag schemes, that specify the types of tags we're interested in. In our case, we want to identify the lexical class of the words in a text. Thus, the tag array will only contain a single element with the tag scheme `.lexicalClass`.

```
    private static let tagger = NLTagger(tagSchemes: [.lexical-
Class])
```

The `.lexicalClass` tag scheme lets us find out whether a token is a part of speech, punctuation, or whitespace.

Let's go back to the `partsOfSpeech(for text: String)` method and initialize the result which is an array that holds `WordLexicalClassPair` objects:

```
    public class func partsOfSpeech(for text: String) -> [WordLex-
icalClassPair] {
        var result = [WordLexicalClassPair]()
```

Then, set the tagger's string property to the text we want to analyze:

```
        tagger.string = text
```

We use the `enumerateTags()` method to retrieve the tokens from a given range of the string. The first parameter is the range to analyze. Since we want to parse the entire string, the range should start at the first index (`text.startIndex`) and should end before the last index (`<text.endIndex`).

```
tagger.enumerateTags(in: text.startIndex..<text.endIndex
```

The next argument is the linguistic unit. Use `NLTokenUnit.word` to enumerate for words.

```
tagger.enumerateTags(in: text.startIndex..<text.endIndex,
    unit: NLTokenUnit.word,
```

Use `NLTagScheme.lexicalClass` for the tag scheme, and include `NLTagger.Options.omitPunctuation` and `NLTagger.Options.omitWhitespace` in the options argument to omit white spaces and punctuation tokens.

```
    scheme: NLTagScheme.lexicalClass,
    options: [.omitPunctuation, .omitWhitespace])
{ (tag, range) -> Bool in
```

The last parameter is a block that's applied to ranges of the string. The block has a tag argument that provides the linguistic tag and a `range` argument, which gives the range of the tag.

Next, instantiate a `WordLexicalClassPair` instance for each detected word. The `range` argument lets us retrieve the word at the given position.

```
{ (tag, range) -> Bool in
    let wordLexicalClass =
        WordLexicalClassPair(word: String(text[range]),
                    lexicalClass: (tag?.rawValue ?? "unknown"))
```

The `lexicalClass`'s textual representation is the returned tag's `rawValue`. If the tag is nil, we assign "unknown" to the lexical class. Then, append the `WordLexicalClassPair` instance to the result array:

```
    result.append(wordLexicalClass)
```

The block's final argument is a reference to a Boolean value. Return true to continue processing the set. If we returned false from within the block, `enumerateTags()` would stop the processing.

```
    return true
}
```

And we return the result:

```
    return result
}
```

Here, we're done with our façade. To test it, switch to the NLPFacadeDemo page and declare a `text` constant:

```
let text = "The Façade is simple yet useful"
print(text)
```

First, we determine the string's language:

```
let language = NLPFacade.dominantLanguage(for: text)  ?? "unknown"
print(language)
```

Next, call the `partsOfSpeech(for:)` method to tokenize the string and find the lexical class for each word in this sentence:

```
let result = NLPFacade.partsOfSpeech(for: text)
print(result)
```

If you run the playground, the console output will show that our class detected the language accurately. It also managed to identify the parts of speech correctly.

```
The Façade is simple yet useful
en
["The": Determiner, "Façade": Noun, "is": Verb, "simple": Adjec-
tive, "yet": Adverb, "useful": Adjective]
```

Most importantly, we have a façade that simplifies the usage of the `NaturalLanguage` framework. We could extract it to a library and reuse it in any project.

You can use the Façade to create wrappers like this that make it easier to work with frequently used components.

The beauty of the Façade pattern becomes evident if we compare the amount of code required to achieve the functionality that we made available via two straightforward methods.

10.3 Conclusion

The Façade wraps one or more components and provides a simpler, easier-to-use interface. Clients can use the features through a simpler API.

Another benefit of the Façade is that it isolates the changes of the underlying types from the callers, so the client code must not be refactored when the wrapped types change.

Use the Façade pattern to simplify the usage of complicated, poorly designed interfaces—or when adding a convenience layer makes sense.

A correctly implemented Façade pattern lets clients use the common features of the wrapped subsystem without directly accessing the underlying types.

11. THE FLYWEIGHT

11.1 Overview

Purpose

The Flyweight pattern saves memory and reduces the creation costs for similar objects that rely on the same immutable data. The Flyweight pattern minimizes memory usage by sharing common data among multiple objects.

To make it work, we have to separate the parts that can change from the immutable set of properties. The unchanging parts get stored in the Flyweight and are protected from changes.

We extract the properties that might change. The clients can manage these mutable properties and pass them to the Flyweight object when necessary.

> The shared, immutable part is called intrinsic state and the properties that can change represent the extrinsic state of the object.

Here's an example to illustrate the process of identifying the extrinsic and intrinsic state. In computer games, we often see objects that look similar: plants, rocks, buildings, vehicles, and so on.

Let's take a concrete case, a spaceship. We can have a fleet of similar ships. They have the same geometry and texture, but their position is different, and it may change. Thus, we can say that the spaceship's mesh and texture are its intrinsic, immutable state. But the ships don't share the same position or speed; besides, these parameters can change. They thus belong to the extrinsic, mutable state.

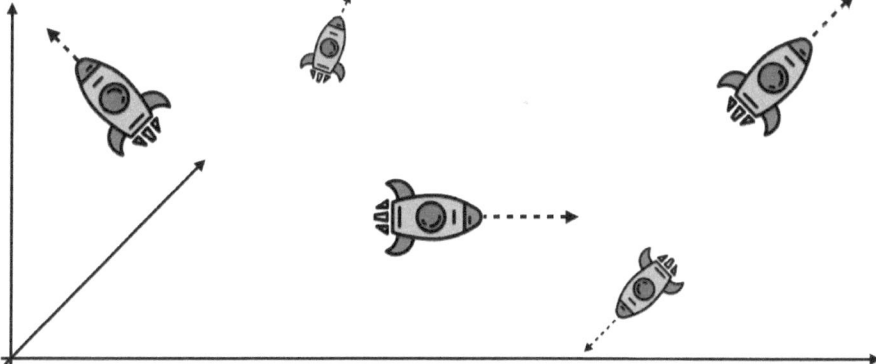

As a consequence, we embed the mesh and the texture into the Flyweight, whereas the spaceship's position and speed should be treated as the extrinsic state.

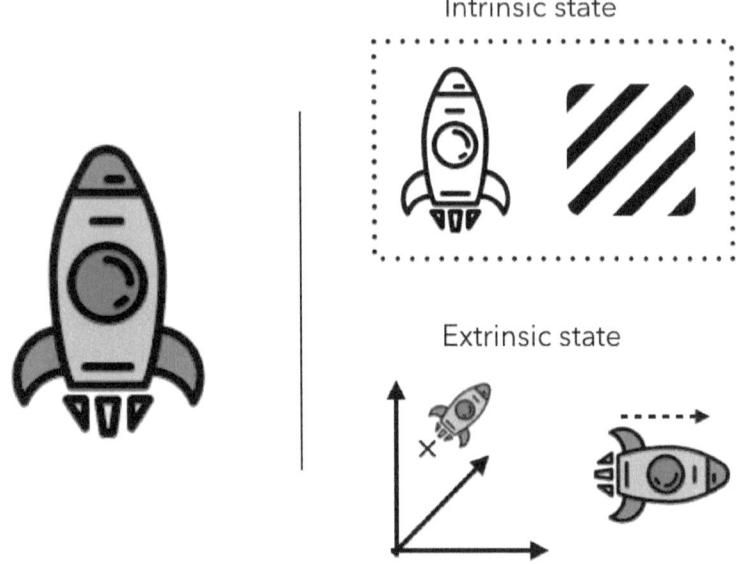

Intrinsic state

Extrinsic state

We're going to highlight the benefits of the Flyweight by refactoring an unoptimized example.

Cons of the Flyweight

When implementing the Flyweight pattern, you need to ensure that there's only one intrinsic state object. You can achieve that by applying the Singleton design pattern or by introducing a Flyweight factory that always returns the shared state instance.

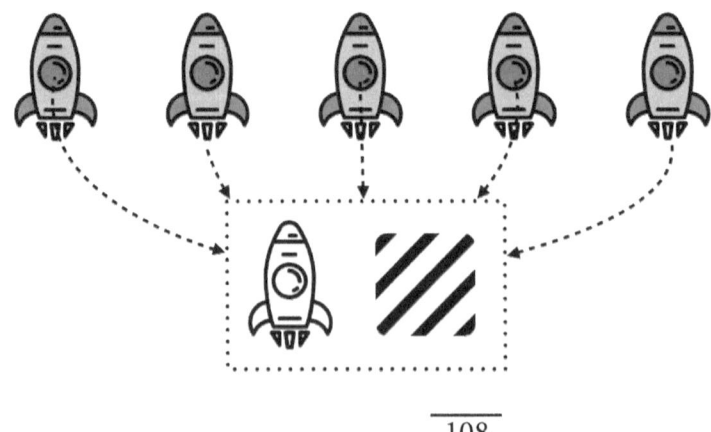

Another issue is accidentally allowing clients to change the immutable state of the Flyweight. Callers must not modify the intrinsic state of the Flyweight object.

11.2 Spaceship Demo

In this section, we're going to optimize a simple `SpaceShip` class using the Flyweight pattern. Create a Swift playground project called Spaceships and define the following class:

```
class SpaceShip {
    private let mesh: [Float]
    private let texture: UIImage?
    private var position: (Float, Float, Float)

    init(mesh: [Float], imageNamed name: String, position: (Float,
Float, Float) = (0, 0, 0)) {
        self.mesh = mesh
        self.texture = UIImage(named: name)
        self.position = position
    }
}
```

Each `SpaceShip` has a `mesh` of polygons that describe its geometry. It also has a `texture` that makes it look realistic and a `position` provided as coordinates in 3D space.

Normally, we would use SceneKit to represent 3D entities. We're only using this example to illustrate the problem solved by the Flyweight pattern.

The following snippet creates 1000 starships:

```
let fleetSize = 1000
var ships = [SpaceShip]()
var vertices = [Float](repeating: 0, count: 1000) // just a dummy
array of floats

for _ in 0..<fleetSize {
    let ship = SpaceShip(mesh: vertices,
            imageNamed: "SpaceShip",
            position: (Float.random(in: 1...100),
                    Float.random(in: 1...100),
                    Float.random(in: 1...100)))
    ships.append(ship)
}
```

The mesh and the texture can be quite large for a detailed model. Creating a fleet might cause all sorts of problems, including memory issues and low performance.

If the mesh data is 100kB in size and the texture is, say, 200kB, creating 1000 SpaceShip instances would require more than 300 MB of memory.

We can do better than that! Let's apply the Flyweight pattern.

First, we need to identify the intrinsic state; that is, the set of data that can be shared between objects.

All the ships use the same mesh and texture, and we have them in memory 1000 times. We can definitely share this data between the SpaceShip instances.

```
for _ in 0..<fleetSize {
    let ship = SpaceShip(mesh: vertices, imageNamed: "SpaceShip",
```

What about the position property? Should all ships share the same position? That doesn't sound like a good idea. The position property shouldn't be shared, as it needs to be different for each SpaceShip object.

Now that we have identified the intrinsic and the extrinsic state, we can go ahead and implement the flyweight pattern.

Extract the mesh and the texture to a separate class. It's important to declare it as a class because we need a reference type—I'll explain this in a moment.

Let's call the class SharedSpaceShipData and copy the mesh and the texture properties from the original class:

```
class SharedSpaceShipData {
    private let mesh: [Float]
    private let texture: UIImage?
```

We need an initializer:

```
    init(mesh: [Float], imageNamed name: String) {
        self.mesh = mesh
        self.texture = UIImage(named: name)
    }
```

Now, we can remove the mesh and the texture properties from the SpaceShip class. We keep only the position property:

```
class SpaceShip {
    //private let mesh: [Float]
    //private let texture: UIImage?
    private var position: (Float, Float, Float)
```

Add a property of type SharedSpaceShipData:

```
private var intrinsicState: SharedSpaceShipData
```

Next, refactor the initializer. Let's get rid of the `mesh` and the `imageNamed` parameters:

```
init(/*mesh: [Float], imageNamed name: String,*/ position:
(Float, Float, Float) = (0, 0, 0)) {
```

Also add a new argument called `sharedData` of type `SharedSpaceShipData`.

```
init(/*mesh: [Float], imageNamed name: String,*/ sharedData:
SharedSpaceShipData, position: (Float, Float, Float) = (0, 0, 0))
{
```

Now, we can remove the mesh and the texture initialization part. Then, initialize the intrinsic state:

```
init(/*mesh: [Float], imageNamed name: String,*/ sharedData:
SharedSpaceShipData, position: (Float, Float, Float) = (0, 0, 0))
{
    //self.mesh = mesh
    //self.texture = UIImage(named: name)
    self.intrinsicState = sharedData
    self.position = position

}
```

To create the fleet, we need to instantiate a `SharedSpaceShipData` object first:

```
let sharedState = SharedSpaceShipData(mesh: vertices, imageNamed:
"SpaceShip")
```

Then, create 1000 `SpaceShip` objects in a loop. Each instance gets a reference to the shared, intrinsic state.

```
for _ in 0..<fleetSize {
    let ship = SpaceShip(sharedData: sharedState,
            position: (Float.random(in: 1...100),
                Float.random(in: 1...100),
                Float.random(in: 1...100)))
    ships.append(ship)
}
```

Thus, instead of having the same polygon mesh and texture data loaded one thousand times in memory, we have one thousand `SpaceShip` objects that hold a reference to a single `SharedSpaceShipData` instance.

The type that represents the intrinsic state needs to be a reference type: that's why we declared `SharedSpaceShipData` as a class. This limitation is required to avoid the copying of instances.

If we declared the `SharedSpaceShipData` as a value type (e.g., as a structure or an enum) it would be automatically copied upon assignment. That's not the behavior we want, as it would produce the same problem we're trying to solve.

The Flyweight design pattern helped us reduce the memory requirements and the creation costs of objects significantly.

You can apply this design pattern whenever you need to create several objects that share a common set of immutable properties.

11.3 Conclusion

The Flyweight pattern should be applied to create large amounts of similar objects that rely on the same set of immutable data. The memory usage is reduced by sharing common data among objects.

To implement the Flyweight pattern, we must separate the immutable set of properties from the state-dependent part. A reference to the intrinsic, shared state gets stored in the Flyweight object, whereas the state-dependent, extrinsic state is managed by clients and passed to the Flyweight when required.

12. THE PROXY

12.1 Overview

Purpose

The Proxy software design pattern is about managing and controlling access to specific objects. The proxy acts as a placeholder for the proxied instance; it introduces an additional level of indirection to support controlled, remote, or delayed access.

Why would we need that additional level of indirection? There are certain situations when providing a surrogate is a better choice than accessing the object directly:

1. The object is a resource hog, and you want to delay its creation until it's first accessed. We'll use the virtual proxy to address this problem.

2. You rely on a remote resource, like a web service.
   The remote proxy acts as a local placeholder to control and optimize access to the real resource. For example, a remote proxy may batch network calls before accessing a RESTful service or return cached data instead of firing a network request.

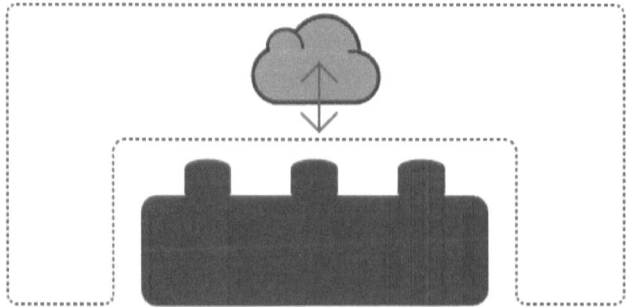

3. You use protected or sensitive resources.
   The protective proxy ensures that the caller has the appropriate

permissions to access the component. It can expose methods to authenticate users or query the access state.

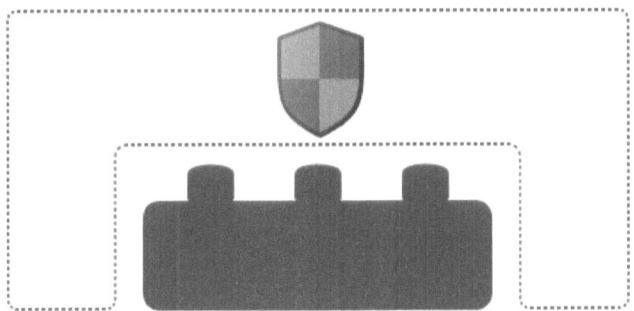

Cons of the Proxy

The Proxy must not allow clients to use the proxied type directly. In other words, the underlying type needs to be hidden, and clients should only be able to use the proxy object.

The benefits of the proxy pattern are rendered useless if clients can bypass the surrogate and use the underlying types directly.

12.2 The Virtual Proxy

The virtual proxy can be used to minimize the costs of creating expensive objects.

Swift lazy properties provide a convenient way to implement the virtual proxy pattern. Our aim is to delay the creation of objects until they are actually used.

In this example, we'll create an image proxy class. Start a new playground project called VirtualImageProxy and import the UIKit and the PlaygroundSupport frameworks:

```
import UIKit
import PlaygroundSupport
```

Then, define the RemoteImage protocol; it declares a couple of properties and an initializer:

```
public protocol RemoteImage: CustomStringConvertible {
    init(url: URL)
    var image: UIImage? { get }
    var url: URL { get }
    var hasContent: Bool { get }
}
```

Let's continue with the implementation class. The ImageProxy class conforms to the RemoteImage protocol, so we need to define the initializer and the properties declared by the protocol. The url and hasContent properties are straightforward:

```
public class ImageProxy: RemoteImage {
    public let url: URL
    public var hasContent: Bool = false
```

The initializer sets the url property:

```
required public init(url: URL) {
    self.url = url
}
```

Let's take a closer look at the image property.

```
public lazy var image: UIImage? = {
}()
```

Swift provides an elegant way to implement the virtual proxy pattern. The lazy
keyword makes sure that the property is only set when it is accessed for the
first time. We can assign a value to a lazy property, or we can use a closure if
more initialization steps are needed.

```
public lazy var image: UIImage? = { [unowned self] in
    var result: UIImage?
    if let img = try? UIImage(data: Data(contentsOf: self.
url)) {
        result = img
        self.hasContent = true
    }
    return result
}()
```

The image is constructed from a Data instance, which in turn is initialized with
the contents of a URL. This method call may throw an error. To keep it simple
we use conditional try? to handle potential errors; if an error is thrown, try?
discards it and returns nil.

If a closure is assigned to a property of a class instance, and we refer to the
instance or any of its members from within the closure's scope, then the
closure captures the instance. This creates a strong reference cycle between
the closure and the instance. A strong reference cycle causes objects to own
each other. Each object ensures that the other stays alive. Therefore, they will
never be deallocated.

In our case, the ImageProxy class owns the closure through the image property.
And the closure also owns self, since we refer to self in the closure. Swift uses
capture lists to break these strong reference cycles. The unowned keyword
prevents the closure from owning the instance, so we don't create a strong
reference cycle anymore.

```
public lazy var image: UIImage? = { [unowned self] in
    //...
}()
```

Use unowned `self` only when `self` is known to be around when the closure code gets executed. Otherwise, use weak `self`.

Next, we add a custom description to our virtual proxy via a protocol extension. Protocol extensions allow us to define behavior on the protocol itself rather than in each conforming type.

```
extension RemoteImage: CustomStringConvertible {
    public var description: String {
        let description = hasContent ? "Image available. Retrieved
from \(self.url.absoluteString)" : "No image available yet!"
        return description
    }
}
```

We can now try out our virtual proxy.

```
guard let imageURL = URL(string: "https://developer.apple.com/
swift/images/swift-og.png") else {
    fatalError("Could not create URL")
}

let imageProxy = ImageProxy(url: imageURL)

print(imageProxy)
```

After creating the `imageProxy` object, the image property should be empty; this is confirmed by the log output in the console.

```
No image available yet!
```

We must first access the `image` property to download the resource.

```
let image = imageProxy.image
print(imageProxy)
```

The console output becomes:

```
Image available. Retrieved from https://developer.apple.com/swift/
images/swift-og.png
```

That's precisely the behavior we aimed for with our virtual proxy implementation.

As a bonus, lazy properties get initialized only once. To prove this, we can increment a counter in the closure.

```
public class ImageProxy: RemoteImage {
```

```
// ...

private var counter = 0

// ...

public lazy var image: UIImage? = { [unowned self] in
    self.counter += 1
    print("image property accessed \(self.counter) time(s)")

    // ...

    return result
}()
}
```

We then access the `image` property ten times from a loop.

```
for _ in 1...10 {
    imageProxy.image
}
```

The console output shows that the `image` property has been accessed only one time:

```
image property accessed 1 time(s)
```

The `ImageProxy` does a great job at deferring expensive object creation until callers really need the resource.

12.3 The Remote Proxy

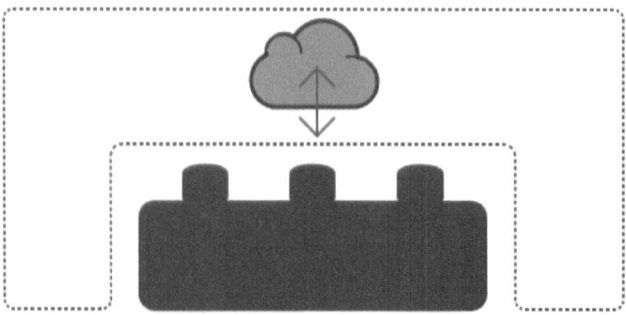

The Remote Proxy minimizes the costs of accessing resources that require expensive operations, like network calls.

The proxy can perform under-the-hood optimizations like doing batch calls or deferring the invocation of slow or computationally exhaustive operations until performing them is required.

In the following example, we are going to implement a Remote Proxy. HTTP requests are expensive when it comes to execution time, bandwidth, and energy usage. The Remote Proxy decouples the execution of the expensive call from the use of remote data. In addition, we do not expose any details of how the network is used, which isolates callers from future changes in the proxy implementation.

Create a new playground project and name it RemoteProxy.

Import the `Foundation` and the `PlaygroundSupport` frameworks:

```
import Foundation
import PlaygroundSupport
```

We start by defining the `RemoteData` protocol, which declares two methods.

```
public protocol RemoteData {
    public func data(url: URL,
        completionHandler: @escaping(Error?, Data?) -> Void) ->
RemoteData {
    func run()
}
```

The `data(url:, completionHandler:)` method's first parameter is the URL of the remote resource. The completion handler returns either a valid data reference or an error.

The purpose of the `run()` method is to execute the remote call, which is required to fetch the payload from the resource URL.

Note that the `data(url:, completionHandler:)` method returns a `RemoteData` instance, which allows callers to chain the calls to the `data(url:, completionHandler:)` and `run()` methods together. This syntax is known as method cascading.

Next, we implement the `RemoteDataProxy` class. The `data(url:, completionHandler:)` method doesn't do much in particular: it stores the URL and the completion handler in corresponding private properties.

```
public class RemoteDataProxy: RemoteData {
    fileprivate var callback: ((Error?, Data?) -> Void)?
    fileprivate var url: URL?

    public init() {}

    public func data(url: URL,
        completionHandler: @escaping(Error?, Data?) -> Void) ->
RemoteData {
        self.url = url
        self.callback = completionHandler
        return self
    }
```

The real work is done in the `run()` method:

```
    public func run() {
        if let callback = self.callback, let url = self.url {
```

We rely on `URLSession` for networking. The task executes asynchronously, and the completion block gets invoked when the task completes.

```
            URLSession.shared.dataTask(with: url) { (data, re-
sponse, error) in
```

We implement some basic error handling.

```
                guard let data = data,
                    error == nil else {
                    print("Could not download data from URL \(url.
absoluteString). Reason: \(error!.localizedDescription)")
                    callback(error, nil)
                    return
                }
```

Then, we invoke the caller's completion handler that was provided in the `data(url:, completionHandler:)` method and stored in the `callback` private property.

```
                print("Data successfully fetched from URL \(url.
absoluteString)")
                callback(nil, data)
            }.resume()

        print("Downloading data from URL \(url.absolut-
eString)")
        } else {
            print("run() called before invoking data(url: comple-
tionHandler:")
        }
    }
}
```

The caller components can use our remote proxy by instantiating a `RemoteDataProxy` object. The client code should include calls to the `data(url:, completionHandler:)` method in places where remote data is used. As a reminder: there is no network operation involved at this point yet.

```
guard let dataURL = URL(string: "https://developer.apple.com/
swift/images/swift-og.png") else {
    fatalError("Could not create URL")
}

let dataProxy = RemoteDataProxy().data(url: dataURL) { (error,
data) in
    guard error == nil else {
        print("Could not retrieve data from URL \(dataURL.absolut-
eString)")
        return
    }

    print("\(data?.count ?? 0) bytes retrieved from URL \(dataURL.
absoluteString)")
}
```

The client code can trigger a call to the `run()` method when the remote data is indeed needed.

```
// deferred execution
dataProxy.run()
```

This is a much better approach than fetching the data right away as there might be cases when the remote data is not used at all.

By default, the playground won't wait for the asynchronous call to complete.

The execution stops right after calling the `run()` method, which returns almost instantly. We need to enable indefinite playground execution which gives enough time for the asynchronous code to execute.

```
PlaygroundPage.current.needsIndefiniteExecution = true
```

The console shows the result of the deferred image download:

```
Downloading data from URL https://developer.apple.com/swift/imag-
es/swift-og.png

Data successfully fetched from URL https://developer.apple.com/
swift/images/swift-og.png

25513 bytes retrieved from URL https://developer.apple.com/swift/
images/swift-og.png
```

12.4 Protective Proxy

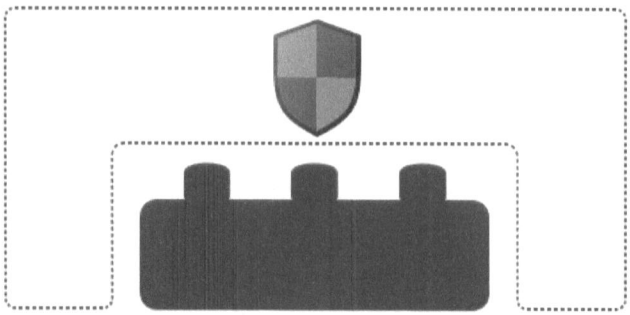

The protective proxy controls access to a sensitive resource. The proxy wraps the protected object and performs certain permission checks before forwarding the requests to the real object.

Let's implement a protective proxy which restricts access to the `ImageProxy` we created previously.

First, we need to define a type that performs the access checks. The `Authenticating` protocol declares the `isAuthenticated` read-only property and a method to authenticate the user.

```
public protocol Authenticating {
    var isAuthenticated: Bool {get}
    func authenticate(user: String) -> Bool
}
```

The `Authenticator` class implements a very basic way to "authenticate" users: it simply checks if the provided username matches any of the names contained in the `userWhiteList` array.

```
public class Authenticator: Authenticating {
    static public let shared = Authenticator()
    public var isAuthenticated: Bool = false
    fileprivate let userWhiteList = ["John", "Mary", "Steve"]
    fileprivate let syncQueue = DispatchQueue(label: "com.leakka.
authQueue")

    fileprivate init() {}

    public func authenticate(user: String) -> Bool {
        var result = false
        syncQueue.sync {
            result = userWhiteList.contains(user) ? true : false
```

```
            if result == false {
                print("Error: Unauthorized!")
                isAuthenticated = false
            } else {
                print("Authorized!")
                isAuthenticated = true
            }
        }
        return result
    }
}
```

Clients can use the shared `Authenticator` instance to authenticate users or query the access state.

Next, we define the `SecureImageProxy` class.

```
public class SecureImageProxy: RemoteImage {
    public let url: URL
    public var hasContent: Bool = false
    fileprivate lazy var imageProxy: ImageProxy = ImageProxy(url:
self.url)

    required public init(url: URL) {
        self.url = url
    }
}
```

It implements the `RemoteImage` protocol—the same protocol as the type it is wrapping—which allows callers to use the protective proxy as a replacement for the wrapped object.

Now let's have a look at the implementation of the `image` property:

```
    required public init(url: URL) {
        self.url = url
    }
    public var image: UIImage? {
        get {
            return Authenticator.shared.isAuthenticated ? self.
imageProxy.image : nil
        }
    }
}
```

If the user is authorized, we access the `imageProxy` and query its `image` property. Otherwise, we return nil.

Note that the `imageProxy` is a lazy variable itself:

```
     fileprivate lazy var imageProxy: ImageProxy = ImageProxy(url:
self.url)
```

Therefore, its instantiation is deferred until we first access it.

The `SecureImageProxy` restricts access to the underlying `ImageProxy` object. Clients are supposed to use the protective proxy rather than accessing the protected resource directly.

To prevent bypassing the `SecureImageProxy`, we change the access level of the `ImageProxy` class from `public` to `private`:

```
private class ImageProxy: RemoteImage {}
```

Now we have a simple, yet functional protective proxy. Let's do some testing:

```
guard let imageURL = URL(string: "https://developer.apple.com/
swift/images/swift-og.png") else {
    fatalError("Could not create URL")
}

let secureImageProxy = SecureImageProxy(url: imageURL)
print(secureImageProxy)

Authenticator.shared.authenticate(user: "Jim")
if secureImageProxy.image != nil {
    print("Proxy has a valid image")
}

Authenticator.shared.authenticate(user: "John")
if secureImageProxy.image != nil {
    print("Proxy has a valid image")
}

PlaygroundPage.current.needsIndefiniteExecution = true
```

The console output shows that the protective proxy does its job:

```
No image available yet!
Error: Unauthorized!
Authorized!
image property accessed 1 time(s)
Proxy has a valid image
```

12.5 Conclusion

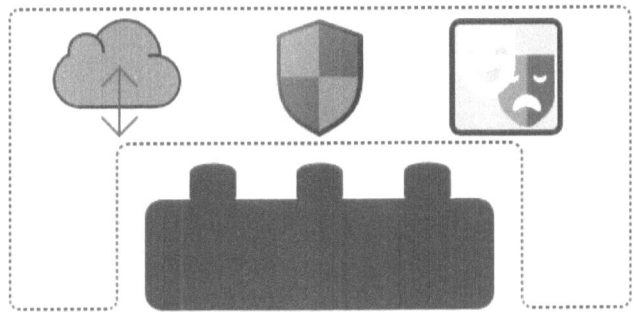

You can use the proxy pattern in the following situations:

→ To access remote resources like RESTful services.
The remote proxy acts as a local placeholder for a remote object; clients can call methods of this local representative which in turn forwards the requests to the remote object.

→ To manage the creation of expensive resources and the execution of computationally intensive operations.
We can improve performance and memory usage by postponing the creation of expensive resources until they are first accessed.

→ To control access to sensitive objects.
The surrogate object checks whether the caller has the appropriate permissions required to use the protected resource.

The proxy object should be used to perform all the required operations on the resource it represents.

13. THE CHAIN OF RESPONSIBILITY

13.1 Overview

Purpose

The Chain of Responsibility design pattern decouples the sender of a request from its potential receivers. The receivers form a chain, and the request travels

The first object receives the request; if it's not interested in the specific request, it forwards it to the next receiver. The request travels until one of the objects processes the request, or until we reach the end of the chain.

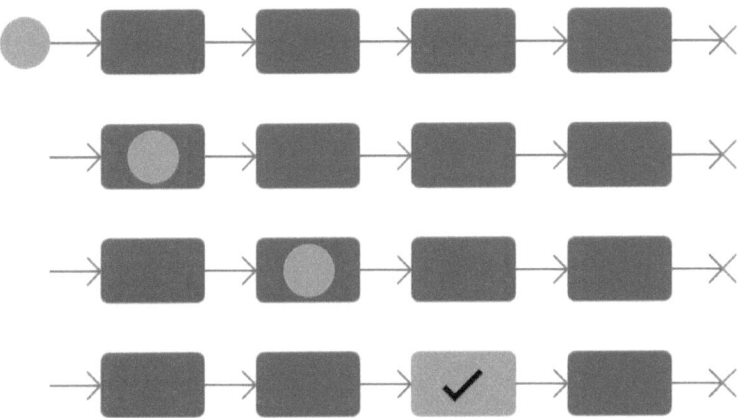

The chain is implemented as a singly linked list, with each receiver holding a reference to its successor in the chain. The end of the chain is either a nil reference or a reference to a special type.

We can manage the chain of responders dynamically by adding new responders or removing existing ones from the list.

In some cases, the responder may forward the request through the chain after it handles it. This approach lets multiple responders process the same request.

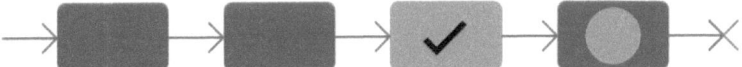

This is how iOS or Mac OS handle mouse clicks and taps on the user interface. The Chain of Responsibility stands at the core of user event processing in Cocoa and Cocoa Touch.

Pitfalls

The Chain of Responsibility is a popular pattern that can address various problems that require passing the request between objects organized in a sequence.

However, you shouldn't use it when each request is only handled by one responder, or when the number of request handlers is very limited.

13.2 Message Processing Demo

In this demo, we're going to implement a chain of handlers that can process specific request types.

Start Xcode and create a Swift playground project called MessageProcessing.

We start with the `RequestHandling` protocol that defines the interface that all request handlers need to adopt.

```
protocol RequestHandling {
```

The protocol declares an initializer that takes an argument of type `RequestHandling`. This parameter represents the next responder in the chain. It's optional, so callers can also pass in nil to mark the end of the chain.

```
    init(next: RequestHandling?)
```

Next, we declare the method responsible for processing a specific request.

```
    func handle(request: Any)
```

The method can take any type as argument. If a concrete responder doesn't deal with a particular request, it must forward it to the next responder.

Next, we'll implement a type that adopts the `RequestHandling` protocol. Instead of creating multiple concrete types, we're going to define a generic `Handler` class with a type parameter called `T`. We declare it as a final class to prevent the creation of subclasses:

```
final class Handler<T>
```

Let's make it conform to the `RequestHandling` protocol.

```
final class Handler<T>: RequestHandling {
```

Next, declare a private property called `nextHandler` of type optional `RequestHandling`:

```
    private var nextHandler: RequestHandling?
```

The `nextHandler` property references the next responder. If it's nil, it denotes the end of the responder chain.

The `RequestHandling` protocol conformance requires us to implement the initializer and the `handle(request:)` method. Let's start with the initializer—it simply sets the `nextHandler` property:

```
init(next: RequestHandling?) {
    self.nextHandler = next
}
```

Next comes the `handle(request:)` method:

```
func handle(request: Any) {
```

It first checks if the request's type matches the type our handler can process:

```
if request is T {
    print("Request processed by \(self)")
} else {
```

If the handler processes the request, we print a message to the console. Otherwise, we check if there's a valid next handler in the chain. If `nextHandler` is nil, we print that we reached the end of the responder chain and return.

```
guard let handler = nextHandler else {
    print("Reached the end of the responder chain.")
    return
}
```

If `nextHandler` references a valid object, we print a log message telling that the current handler can't handle the request, and we forward it to the next handler by calling its `handle(request:)` method.

```
        print("\(self) can't handle \(type(of: request)) re-
quests - forwarding to \(handler)")
        handler.handle(request: request)
```

Finally, add a custom description by making the `Handler` class conform to the `CustomStringConvertible` protocol:

```
final class Handler<T>: RequestHandling, CustomStringConvertible {
```

We need to implement the description property to make our type conform to the `CustomStringConvertible` protocol. The description provides which request type is processed by the given handler:

```
public var description: String {
    return "\(T.self) Handler"
}
```

Let's build the chain of handlers; we start with the last handler, and we're going to add the other responders progressively. The last handler object can handle requests of type `Data`. It has no next responder, so pass in nil to its initializer:

```
```

```
let dataHandler = Handler<Data>(next: nil)
```

Next, create a `String` handler instance and set its next responder to the `dataHandler` instance:

```
let stringHandler = Handler<String>(next: dataHandler)
```

And here's the third handler: `dateHandler` works with `Date` types, and its next responder is the `stringHandler` instance:

```
let dateHandler = Handler<Date>(next: stringHandler)
```

We have three handlers in our chain: a `Date`, a `String`, and a `Data` handler. If the `dateHandler` can't handle the request, it forwards it to the `stringHandler`. And if the `stringHandler` can't process the request either, our last chance is the `dataHandler`.

Create a `Data` instance and pass it to the `dataHandler`'s `handle(request:)` method:

```
let data = Data(repeating: 0, count: 10)
dataHandler.handle(request: data)
```

The console shows the expected outcome:

```
Request processed by Data Handler
```

Now let's see what happens if we pass the `Data` instance to the `dateHandler`:

```
dataHandler.handle(request: data)
```

The console log reveals how the request gets forwarded until the `Data` handler processes it:

```
Date Handler can't handle Data requests - forwarding to String
Handler
String Handler can't handle Data requests - forwarding to Data
Handler
Request processed by Data Handler
```

Finally, let's use a data type that's not handled by any of the handlers.

```
dateHandler.handle(request: 42)
```

There are no `Int` processors in the chain; therefore, we reach the end of the chain of responders without handling the request:

```
Date Handler can't handle Int requests - forwarding to String Han-
```

```
dler
String Handler can't handle Int requests - forwarding to Data Han-
dler
Reached the end of the responder chain
```

13.3 Backup Service Demo

Let's assume that we want to create a framework for retrieving weather information. We'll have to rely on web services to fetch live data from the internet.

Web services can be unreliable at times. To maximize our chances, we're going to use multiple services. We'll use a fallback strategy: if a service is unavailable or if it reports an error, we will automatically switch to the next one.

Create a playground project called BackupService.

First, define the `WeatherService` protocol. The protocol is `fileprivate` as we don't want clients to use it directly. We're going to expose a public wrapper instead.

`WeatherService` declares a read-only property called `backupService`. This property plays a key role in our fallback strategy.

```
fileprivate protocol WeatherService {
    var backupService: WeatherService? { get }
```

The `backupService` computed property is optional: a nil value indicates that there's no backup service.

The `WeatherService` protocol declares the `fetchCurrentWeather(city:, countryCode:, completionHandler:)` method for retrieving weather data. The method takes two arguments: the `city` and the `countryCode`.

```
    func fetchCurrentWeather(city: String, countryCode: String,
completionHandler: (WeatherData?, WeatherServiceError?) -> Void)
```

The third argument is the completion handler that will return either the valid weather data or an error.

Next, we need to define the `WeatherData` structure. It declares the most important properties describing the weather.

```
public struct WeatherData {
    public let city: String
    public let country: String
    public let weather: String
    public let temp: Float
    public let unit: TempUnit
}
```

We represent the temperature units through the `TempUnit` enumeration that defines three cases: `scientific`, `metric`, and `imperial`.

```
public enum TempUnit {
    case scientific
    case metric
    case imperial
}
```

Next, assign the appropriate descriptions via a type extension which implements the `CustomStringConvertible` protocol.

```
extension TempUnit: CustomStringConvertible {
    public var description: String {
        switch self {
        case .scientific:
            return "Kelvin"
        case .metric:
            return "Celsius"
        case .imperial:
            return "Fahrenheit"
        }
    }
}
```

Next, we create the concrete types that implement the `WeatherService` protocol.

Note that we won't rely on real web services. We aim to illustrate the Chain of Responsibility design pattern rather than implementing a fully-formed weather application. We'll simulate service failures or data validation issues to demonstrate how the fallback system works.

The `WeatherServiceError` enumeration defines the possible issues: service down (`serviceDown`), invalid or missing response (`noData`), and unknown error (`unknown`) for everything else.

```
public enum WeatherServiceError: Error {
    case serviceDown
    case noData
    case unknown
}
```

Let's provide localized error messages by implementing the `LocalizedError` protocol in a type extension. You should always provide meaningful error descriptions.

```
extension WeatherServiceError: LocalizedError {
    public var errorDescription: String? {
        switch self {
        case .serviceDown:
            return "Service unavailable"
        case .noData:
            return "Could not retrieve weather data"
        case .unknown:
            return "Unknown error occurred"
        }
    }
}
```

OpenWeatherService is the first type that implements the WeatherService protocol.

```
fileprivate struct OpenWeatherService: WeatherService, Custom-
StringConvertible {
    var backupService: WeatherService?
```

Implement the initializer which takes an optional WeatherService argument. Here we set the backupService if the caller provided one.

```
    init(backupService: WeatherService? = nil) {
        self.backupService = backupService
    }
```

We apply the fallback strategy in the fetchCurrentWeather(city:, countryCode:, completionHandler:) method.

We simulate errors through the hasError() helper method. If an error occurs, we try to retrieve the weather data using the backup service. If there's no backup service, we print a message and call the completion handler using nil for the weather data and the error instance.

```
    func fetchCurrentWeather(city: String, countryCode: String,
completionHandler: (WeatherData?, WeatherServiceError?) -> Void) {
        guard self.hasError() == nil else {
            if let backupService = self.backupService {
                let error = self.hasError() ?? .unknown
                print("\(self) could not fetch weather data. Rea-
son: \(error.errorDescription ?? "unknown")")
                print("\t Falling back to \(backupService)")

                backupService.fetchCurrentWeather(city: city,
countryCode: countryCode, completionHandler: completionHandler)
            } else {
                print("Backup service not set. Reached the end of
```

```
the fallback chain\n")
                completionHandler(nil, self.hasError())
        }
        return
    }

    print("Weather data successfully fetched using \(self)")
    completionHandler(WeatherData(city: city, countryCode:
countryCode, weather: "Clear", temp: 72, unit: .imperial), nil)
  }
```

The `hasError()` helper method returns a `serviceDown` error. This is just to simulate an error which may also occur in real-world situations.

```
fileprivate func hasError() -> WeatherServiceError? {
    return .serviceDown
}
```

We need to implement the description property to make `OpenWeatherService` conform to the `CustomStringConvertible` protocol:

```
var description: String {
    return "OpenWeatherService"
}
```

The `AccuWeatherService` structure is the next type which implements the `WeatherService` protocol. Everything is the same except that we simulate a `noData` error in this case.

```
fileprivate struct AccuWeatherService: WeatherService, Custom-
StringConvertible {
    var backupService: WeatherService?

    //...

    func hasError() -> WeatherServiceError? {
        return .noData
    }
}
```

The `DarkSkyService` is our third type that conforms to the `WeatherService` protocol.

```
fileprivate struct DarkSkyService: WeatherService, CustomStringCon-
vertible {
    var backupService: WeatherService?
    //...
```

```
    func hasError() -> WeatherServiceError? {
        return nil
    }
}
```

The `hasError()` method returns nil to simulate a successful weather data fetch from the server. We can finally return meaningful weather information to the caller.

Next, we implement a wrapper that performs the required setup and implements the fallback logic. `WeatherServiceWrapper` relies on the three implementation classes—`OpenWeatherService`, `AccuWeatherService`, and `DarkSkyService`—to do the real work.

We build the chain of weather data providers in the initializer. The last provider is the `DarkSkyService` instance. It has no backup service; thus, if it fails, we cannot return weather data to the caller.

Next, we create the `AccuWeatherService` instance and pass in the `DarkSkyService` object to its initializer. The first provider in the chain is an `OpenWeatherService` object. It receives the `AccuWeatherService` instance during its initialization. The chain of services is now complete: we've got three weather providers. If any of them fails, we still have two more to fetch weather information. We've got a solid fallback strategy that would meet the requirements of real-life applications.

```
public struct WeatherServiceWrapper {
    private let rootService: WeatherService

    public init() {
        let darkSkyService = DarkSkyService()
        let accuWeatherService = AccuWeatherService(backupService:
darkSkyService)
        rootService = OpenWeatherService(backupService: accuWeath-
erService)
    }
```

The `WeatherServiceWrapper` exposes a public method to retrieve the weather data for a specific city. The method invokes the `fetchCurrentWeather(city:, countryCode:, completionHandler:)` method of the first object in the chain (`rootService`), which is an `OpenWeatherService` instance.

```
    public func fetchCurrentWeather(city: String, countryCode:
String, completionHandler: (WeatherData?, WeatherServiceError?) ->
Void) {
        rootService.fetchCurrentWeather(city: city, countryCode:
```

```
countryCode) { (weatherData, error) in
        guard error == nil else {
            completionHandler(nil, error)
            return
        }
        completionHandler(weatherData, nil)
    }
  }
}
```

The wrapper hides the actual implementation classes and doesn't expose the fallback strategy. This approach lets us make future changes without affecting the callers.

It's time to test our fallback strategy. Instantiate the wrapper and invoke the `fetchCurrentWeather(city:, countryCode:, completionHandler:)` method.

```
//: The client interacts with the WeatherServiceWrapper instance
let weatherService = WeatherServiceWrapper()
weatherService.fetchCurrentWeather(city: "San Francisco", country-
Code: "US") { (weatherData, error) in
    guard error == nil else {
        print("Error while retrieving weather data: \(error?.er-
rorDescription ?? "")")
        return
    }
    print(weatherData ?? "No weather data")
}
```

You should see the following console output:

```
OpenWeatherService could not fetch weather data. Reason: Service
unavailable
    Falling back to AccuWeatherService
AccuWeatherService could not fetch weather data. Reason: Could not
retrieve weather data
    Falling back to DarkSky
Weather data successfully fetched using DarkSky
WeatherData(city: "San Francisco", countryCode: "US", weather:
"Clear", temp: 72.0, unit: Fahrenheit)
```

The weather data was returned by the `DarkSkyService` instance, as the two preceding services failed to handle the request.

The Chain of Responsibility provides an elegant way of implementing fallback strategies for similar situations.

13.4 Conclusion

The Chain of Responsibility design pattern organizes request processors in a chain. The request gets propagated through the chain until it reaches the end of the chain.

A specific responder may or may not process the request. In some cases, the responder may forward the request to the next responder after it handles it. Thus, multiple responders can process the same request.

The Chain of Responsibility design pattern stands at the core of the responder chain on iOS and macOS. It is a widely used pattern that can solve various problems that require passing the request between objects organized in a sequence.

14. THE ITERATOR

14.1 Overview

Purpose

The Iterator design pattern provides sequential access to the elements of an aggregate object, without exposing the internal details of the traversed object.

Whenever you use the for-in loop to traverse over the elements of a collection, you're relying on the Iterator design pattern. It feels natural to type the following code:

```
let numbers = [0, 1, 2, 3]
for n in numbers {
    //...
}
```

We should be able to provide the same, seamless experience for custom data types like stacks, linked lists, or trees.

The Iterator pattern solves this problem. It provides a standard interface for traversing different types of aggregate objects.

Instead of adding the traversal logic to the data structure itself, the Iterator works by extracting this functionality into a separate type. Thus, it removes this responsibility from the collection type. Besides, we don't need to expose the details of the underlying data structure to iterate through its elements.

The Swift standard library has two protocols that let us implement custom iterators:

→ The Sequence protocol
  Types that provide sequential access to their elements should adopt the Sequence protocol. All built-in collection types—the Array, the Set, and the Dictionary—conform to this protocol. Our custom types must also adopt the Sequence protocol if we need to iterate through their elements.
  Sequence defines a couple of method requirements. The one that is relevant to us is the makeIterator() method. This method creates an iterator that provides access to the elements of the Sequence.

→ The IteratorProtocol
  This protocol provides a unified interface for accessing the items in a sequence one at a time. The next() method advances to the next element in the sequence and returns it.

We're using the given type's iterator whenever we rely on the for-in loop to iterate through its items.

Iterator Pitfalls

A sloppy iterator might affect the overall performance of the system. We should always consider the performance impact of our custom iterator implementations.

14.2 Implementing a Custom Queue

In this section, we implement a custom queue. If you want to follow along with me, create a new playground and name it Queue.

Queues support fast FIFO (first-in, first-out) semantics for adding and retrieving elements. New elements get added to the back of the queue, and we can remove the item least recently appended. Queues don't provide random access to their elements.

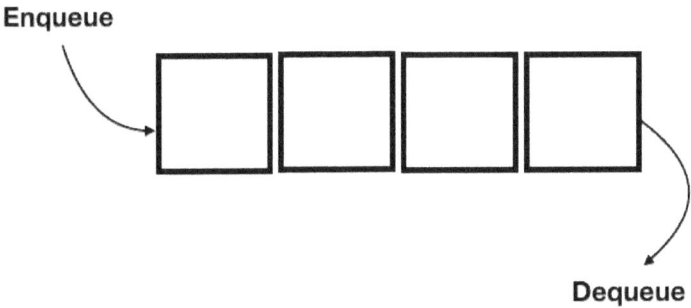

The Node class represents a queue item. The class is generic; thus, it can store any type. It has a property called key of type T?, allowing callers to store any type or a nil value.

The second property is a reference to the next node. Its type is optional (Node?), as newly created nodes don't have a next node.

The initializer sets the key property.

```swift
private final class Node<T> {
    var key: T?
    var next: Node?

    init(_ value: T? = nil) {
        key = value
    }
}
```

The generic Queue class has two methods. The first is enqueue(_:), which appends a new item to the queue.

```swift
final class Queue<T> {
    fileprivate var head: Node<T>?
```

```
    private var tail: Node<T>?

    func enqueue(_ value: T) {
```

First, it creates a new node; then, it checks if the head property has been set.

```
        let newNode = Node<T>(value)
        // First element's value has not been set?
        guard head != nil else {
            head = newNode
            tail = head
            return
        }
```

If the head is nil, that means that our queue was empty. Thus, the new node becomes the head. The tail and the head refer to the same node when the queue has only one element.

If the queue is not empty, we append the new element by setting the tail's next reference to the new node. Finally, the new node becomes the tail of the queue.

```
        // append new element
        tail?.next = newNode
        tail = newNode
    }
```

The dequeue() method returns the top-level item from the queue. The queue works according to the "first-in, first-out" principle, so the least-recently-added item gets returned.

```
    func dequeue() -> T? {
```

We also need to remove the given item from the queue, which requires additional housekeeping. We return nil if the head's key doesn't contain a value.

```
        guard let headItem = head?.key else {
            return nil
        }
```

Otherwise, we check if the head has a valid next node. If it does, we set the head reference to the next node. If the head is the only node in the queue, we set both the head and the tail to nil.

```
        if let nextNode = head?.next {
            head = nextNode
        } else {
            head = nil
            tail = nil
```

```
        }
        return headItem
    }
```

Add two more methods to complete the `Queue` implementation:

→ `isEmpty()` returns true if the head is set to nil

```
    func isEmpty() -> Bool {
        return head == nil
    }
```

→ and `peek()` lets us retrieve the value of the top-level item without removing it from the queue.

```
    func peek() -> T? {
        return head?.key
    }
}
```

We can use the `Queue` as follows:

```
var queue = Queue<Int>()
queue.enqueue(1)
queue.enqueue(2)
print(queue.peek() ?? "n.a.")
print(queue.dequeue() ?? "n.a.")
```

However, if we tried to iterate over its elements using a for-in loop, we'd get a compiler error.

```
// This won't work!
for item in queue {
    print(item)
}
```

We're going to fix that in a moment!

14.3 Adding for-in Loop Support

Let's add support for iterating through the queue's elements using a for-in loop. We're going to implement the Iterator pattern the Swift way.

The Swift standard library exposes two protocols that let us implement the Iterator pattern: `Sequence` and the `IteratorProtocol`.

By adding `Sequence` protocol conformance to our queue, we can create a custom iterator that provides sequential access to its elements. The `IteratorProtocol` should be adopted by the iterator type.

We start with `Sequence` protocol conformance. We adopt the `Sequence` protocol in an extension to avoid cluttering the implementation of the `Queue` class.

```
extension Queue: Sequence {
    func makeIterator() -> QueueIterator<T> {
        return QueueIterator(self)
    }
}
```

The `makeIterator()` method must return an iterator. Create a dedicated `QueueIterator` type that adopts the `IteratorProtocol`:

```
struct QueueIterator<T>: IteratorProtocol {
```

The `QueueIterator` needs to access the queue, so we provide an initializer that takes a parameter of type `Queue`:

```
    init(_ queue: Queue<T>) {}
```

Next, declare two properties that represent the queue and the current node that's returned by the iterator:

```
    private let queue: Queue<T>
    private var currentNode: Node<T>?
```

The initializer sets the properties:

```
    init(_ queue: Queue<T>) {
        self.queue = queue
        currentNode = queue.head
    }
```

The `QueueIterator` needs to implement the `next()` method to conform to the `IteratorProtocol`. The method returns an optional generic type `T?`:

```
    mutating func next() -> T? {
```

Start by validating the current node. If `currentNode` is nil, that means that we either reached the end of the queue or the queue was empty.

```
        guard let node = currentNode else {
            return nil
        }
```

Otherwise, assign the value of the `currentNode`'s key property to a constant. Then, update the `currentNode` property to point to the next node and, finally, return the item.

```
        let nextKey = currentNode?.key
        currentNode = node.next
        return nextKey
    }
```

We can now iterate over the elements of the `Queue` using a for-in loop, as if it were a built-in type:

```
for item in queue {
    print(item)
}
```

The for-in loop uses the `Queue`'s iterator and calls its `next()` method internally to return one element at a time as it advances through the sequence.

So we can replace the for-in snippet with the following code:

```
var queueIterator = queue.makeIterator()
while let item = queueIterator.next() {
    print(item)
}
```

First, we call the queue's `makeIterator()` method to create the iterator. Then, we invoke the iterator's `next()` method in a while loop until we reach the end of the queue.

14.4 Conclusion

The Iterator provides sequential access to the elements of an aggregate object. It encapsulates the operations for different traversals into a dedicated Iterator type. The Iterator must not expose the internal structure of the traversed object.

Swift makes it very easy to implement the Iterator design pattern. Types that provide iterated access to their elements must adopt the `Sequence` protocol. Custom iterator types have to conform to the `IteratorProtocol` protocol.

The iterator must keep track of the traversed elements. Calling its `next()` method returns the current element, and it advances one step in the sequence.

You should always consider the performance impact of your iterator implementation. The `next()` method must not perform slow or computationally intensive operations.

15. THE OBSERVER

15.1 Overview

Purpose

The Observer design pattern provides the means of notifying a group of objects about state changes in another object. The observers subscribe to receive notifications and the subject updates them when its state changes. The observer can then retrieve the relevant state of the subject. This approach avoids the tight coupling between the observers and the subject.

The Observer pattern is implemented correctly if the subject interacts with the observers using a well-defined method, usually called `notify()`. The method is defined in a common protocol and all observers need to conform to that protocol. The subject only knows about the common protocol.

No further implementation details are shared with the subject.

Pitfalls

Make sure to unregister the observers from the subject before releasing them. Otherwise, the subject keeps the reference to the observer instance that should've been destroyed and continues updating it, leading to bugs and unexpected behavior.

15.2 Auction Demo

We'll implement an AuctionDemo playground project to demonstrate the Observer design pattern

We'll have an object that represents the Auctioneer. The Auctioneer updates the Bidders when a new bid is accepted or when the reserve price (the minimum allowable bid) has been met.

Our goal is to keep the auctioneer instance independent from the objects that represent the bidder. Let's start by defining the protocols.

First, we define the `Observer` protocol; it has an `update(notification:)` method that takes an argument of type `Notification`. `Notification` is a placeholder type defined using the `associatedtype` keyword. The conforming classes will provide the concrete type.

```
import Foundation

protocol Observer {
    associatedtype Notification
    func update(notification: Notification)
}
```

Define the `Subject` protocol next. The subject allows observers to register and unregister. So let's add the `attach(observer:)` and `detach(observer:)` methods. These methods will change the state of the instance, so both need to be `mutating`.

```
protocol Subject {
    associatedtype O: Observer
    mutating func attach(observer: O)
    mutating func detach(observer: O)
```

The `Subject` also needs a method to notify the observers.

```
    func notifyObservers()
```

We define the concrete types next. The `Bidder` class has to conform to the `Observer` protocol, so we need to implement the `update(notification:)` method.

```
class Bidder: Observer {
    func update(notification: BidNotification) {}
}
```

The `BidNotification` class has two properties: the `bid` and an optional `message`.

```
struct BidNotification {
    var bid: Float
    var message: String?
}
```

Now we can complete the `update(notification:)` method. Let's print a message that includes the `bid` and the `message` included in the notification.

```
class Bidder: Observer {
    func update(notification: BidNotification) {
        print("\t new bid is:\(notification.bid) \(notification.mes-
sage ?? "")")
    }
}
```

To identify the `Bidder` instances, we add a computed property called `id`; this property uses the `ObjectIdentifier` type to create a unique identifier.

```
class Bidder: Observer {
    var id: Int {
        return ObjectIdentifier(self).hashValue
    }
```

Let's include the `id` in the console log to identify the bidders.

```
    func update(notification: BidNotification) {
        print("\t\(self.id) new bid is:\(notification.bid) \(notifi-
cation.message ?? "")")
    }
}
```

Next, create the `Auctioneer` type. It's a structure that adopts the `Subject` protocol.

```
struct Auctioneer: Subject {
```

Add a private array called `bidders` to store the subscribed observers.

```
    private var bidders = [Bidder]()
```

The `attach(observer:)` method appends new observers to the internal list:

```
    mutating func attach(observer: Bidder) {
        bidders.append(observer)
    }
```

It's counterpart, the `detach(observer:)` method removes an observer from the bidders array.

```
mutating func detach(observer: Bidder) {
    self.bidders = bidders.filter{ $0.id != observer.id }
}
```

The `Array` doesn't have a method to identify and remove a particular item. We rely on the `filter()` method to return a new list that does not contain the input argument.

We need two new properties:

```
private var reservePrice: Float = 0
var bid: Float
```

The `notifyObservers()` method notifies the subscribers by calling their `update(notification:)` method.

```
func notifyObservers() {
```

If the reserve is met, we compose a message, otherwise the message is nil.

```
        let message = bid > reservePrice ? "Reserve met, item
sold" : nil
```

The `notification` contains the bid and the message:

```
        let notification = BidNotification(bid: bid, message: mes-
sage)
```

Finally, invoke the `update(notification:)` method on every subscribed observer:

```
        bidders.forEach { $0.update(notification: notification) }
}
```

We need to enhance the bid property, too. Whenever a new bid is made, we notify the observers:

```
private var currentBid: Float = 0

var bid: Float {
    set {
        currentBid = newValue
        notifyObservers()
    }
    get {
        return currentBid
```

```
        }
    }
```

However, we should consider some edge cases. New bids must be higher than previous ones. If the reserve price is met, the item is sold and we end the auction.

```
    private var currentBid: Float = 0
    private var auctionEnded: Bool = false

    var bid: Float {
        set {
            if auctionEnded {
                print("\nAuction ended. We can't accept new
bids.")
            } else if newValue > currentBid {
                print("\nNew bid $\(newValue) accepted")
                if newValue >= reservePrice {
                    print("Reserve price met! Auction ended.")
                    auctionEnded = true
                }
                currentBid = newValue
                notifyObservers()
            }
        }
        get {
            return currentBid
        }
    }
```

We also need an initializer that lets us set the reserve price and, optionally, the initial bid, too:

```
    init(initialBid: Float = 0, reservePrice: Float) {
        self.bid = initialBid
        self.reservePrice = reservePrice
    }
```

Now let's try out what we've built. Create an auctioneer instance and a couple of bidders.

```
var auctioneer = Auctioneer(reservePrice: 500)

let abby = Bidder()
let julia = Bidder()
let joe = Bidder()
let hans = Bidder()
```

Next, register the bidders with the auctioneer (the subject).

```
auctioneer.attach(observer: abby)
auctioneer.attach(observer: julia)
auctioneer.attach(observer: joe)
auctioneer.attach(observer: hans)
```

Whenever a new bid is set, the auctioneer should notify the observers.

```
auctioneer.bid = 100
auctioneer.bid = 150
auctioneer.bid = 300
auctioneer.bid = 550
```

The console log confirms that the bidder instances got notified each time:

```
New bid $100.0 accepted
    -6414686248375445562 new bid is:100.0
    -3423697941632895586 new bid is:100.0
    -4500970686908862620 new bid is:100.0
    -6807787665791080099 new bid is:100.0

New bid $150.0 accepted
    -6414686248375445562 new bid is:150.0
    -3423697941632895586 new bid is:150.0
    -4500970686908862620 new bid is:150.0
    -6807787665791080099 new bid is:150.0

New bid $300.0 accepted
    -6414686248375445562 new bid is:300.0
    -3423697941632895586 new bid is:300.0
    -4500970686908862620 new bid is:300.0
    -6807787665791080099 new bid is:300.0

New bid $550.0 accepted
Reserve price met! Auction ended.
    -6414686248375445562 new bid is:550.0 Reserve met, item sold
    -3423697941632895586 new bid is:550.0 Reserve met, item sold
    -4500970686908862620 new bid is:550.0 Reserve met, item sold
    -6807787665791080099 new bid is:550.0 Reserve met, item sold
```

Perfect! The auction ends when the bid is higher than the reserve price.

15.3 The NotificationCenter

We're going to refactor the Auction demo. Instead of relying on the classic Observer pattern, we'll use the `NotificationCenter` to broadcast and receive `Notification` instances.

We won't need the `Observer` and the `Subject` protocols, so let's remove them.

```
// protocol Observer {}
// protocol Subject {}
```

Next, get rid of the obsolete protocol conformance from each type.

```
class Bidder: /*Observer*/ {}
struct Auctioneer: /*Subject*/ {}
```

We don't need the `update()` method anymore.

```
class Bidder: Observer {
    var id: Int {
        return ObjectIdentifier(self).hashValue
    }

    /*
    func update(notification: BidNotification) {
        print("\t\(self.id) new bid is:\(notification.bid) \(notifi-
cation.message ?? "")")
    }
    */
}
```

Next, add an initializer that allows the caller to register the instance with the `NotificationCenter`:

```
class Bidder: Observer {
    var id: Int {
        return ObjectIdentifier(self).hashValue
    }

    init() {
        NotificationCenter.default.addObserver(forName: NSNotifica-
tion.Name(BidNotificationNames.bidNotification), object: nil, queue:
nil) { (notification) in
```

The closure gets invoked whenever the notification is received. You can send custom keys and values through the `userInfo` dictionary. We'll use the keys "bid" and "message" to set and retrieve the corresponding values.

```
        if let userInfo = notification.userInfo,
        let bidValue = userInfo["bid"] as? Float,
        let message = userInfo["message"] as? String {
            print("\t\(self.id) new bid is \(bidValue) \(mes-
sage)")
        }
    }
  }
}
```

BidNotificationName is a structure with a type property bidNotification that defines a unique name for our notification:

```
struct BidNotificationNames {
    static let bidNotification = "bidNotification"
}
```

Next, we refactor the Auctioneer to use the NotificationCenter API. First, let's get rid of the methods that were required to conform to the Subject protocol:

```
struct Auctioneer: Subject {
    /*
    mutating func attach(observer: Bidder) {
        bidders.append(observer)
    }

    mutating func detach(observer: Bidder) {
        self.bidders = bidders.filter{ $0.id != observer.id }
    }

    func notifyObservers() {
        //...
    }
    */
```

We don't need the bidders array either:

```
    //private var bidders = [Bidder]()
```

Change the bid computed property to send a notification instead of calling the notifyObservers() method:

```
    var bid: Float {
        set {
            if auctionEnded {
                print("\nAuction ended. We don't accept new
bids.")
            } else if newValue > currentBid {
                print("\nNew bid $\(newValue) accepted")
```

```
                      if newValue >= reservePrice {
                          print("Reserve price met! Auction ended.")
                          auctionEnded = true
                      }
                      currentBid = newValue
                      //notifyObservers()
```

Create a notification with the bid and a custom message, and, finally, call the
NotificationCenter's post() method to send the notification:

```
                  let message = bid > reservePrice ? "Reserve met,
item sold" : ""
                  let notification = Notification(name: Notification.
Name(BidNotificationNames.bidNotification), object: nil, userInfo:
["bid": bid, "message": message])
                      NotificationCenter.default.post(notification)
              }
          }
```

Scroll down to the testing part. We don't need to attach the observers to the
auctioneer anymore, so remove those statements:

```
var auctioneer = Auctioneer(reservePrice: 500)

let abby = Bidder()
let julia = Bidder()
let joe = Bidder()
let hans = Bidder()

//auctioneer.attach(observer: abby)
//auctioneer.attach(observer: julia)
//auctioneer.attach(observer: joe)
//auctioneer.attach(observer: hans)
```

Instead of detaching an observer from the auctioneer, we should use the
removeObserver() NotificationCenter method.

The new, NotificationCenter-based version is shorter and cleaner. In most
cases, you should choose the NotificationCenter to register objects to receive
predefined notifications. NotificationCenter completely removes the coupling
between the subject and the observers. Plus, an object can register itself for
multiple different notifications.

15.4 Conclusion

The Observer design pattern allows objects to subscribe to receive notifications about changes in another object. The notification sender, also known as subject, updates the observers when its state changes.

There is no tight coupling between the subject and the observers. The subject only knows that the receivers have adopted the Observer protocol. No further implementation details are needed.

This loosely coupled design lets us easily add or remove observers. There's no need to modify the subject when creating new observer types. The only requirement is to make the new type conform to the Observer protocol.

The Observer pattern is implemented correctly if the subject only calls the observer's `notify()` method.

16. THE STATE

16.1 Overview

Purpose

The State design pattern is the object-oriented solution to monolithic conditional statements. It can be applied successfully to remove complex conditional logic from a software system.

The conditional behavior gets encapsulated into dedicated types. This approach leads to a more flexible system and makes our code easier to maintain and extend. In addition, incorporating new states or updating existing ones requires less effort.

To apply the State pattern, we first need to identify the steps that change the behavior of an object. After that, we encapsulate the steps into dedicated State types.

Pitfalls

One of the common pitfalls is exposing the states to clients. Clients must not interact with the states directly.

I'm going to illustrate the benefits of the State design pattern by getting rid of complex conditional logic from an existing project.

16.2 Conditional Logic Overload

In this section, I'm going to walk you through the process of refactoring the implementation of an ATM simulator using the State design pattern.

Our aim is to get rid of all the conditional code from the ATM class. The revamped design will be easier to maintain and enhance.

This activity diagram models the simplified flow of an ATM transaction.

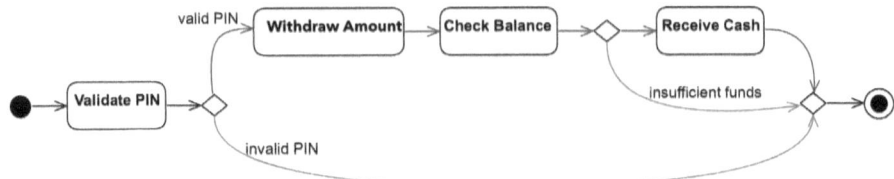

You insert your card, enter your PIN, and if everything goes well, you receive the requested cash.

We start with a Swift playground project called ATMDemo that shows a functional, yet not ideal, way of implementing this flow. Let me briefly explain the code we're about to refactor.

```
import Foundation

public final class ATM {
    private var isPINValid = false
    private var availableFunds: Float = 1000

    public func enter(pin: String) {
        //...
    }

    public func withdraw(amount: Float) -> Bool {
        //...
    }
}
```

The ATM is a public final class. It has two public methods:

→ enter(pin:) which simulates when you're prompted to enter your PIN code after inserting your card.

→ withdraw(amount:) for entering the amount of cash you want to withdraw.

166

The enter(pin:) method performs a basic PIN check. If the provided PIN differs from the predefined value, it displays an error message and exits.

```
public func enter(pin: String) {
    guard pin == "1234" else {
        print("INVALID PIN")
        print("Transaction Failed... don't forget your card!")
        return
    }
```

Otherwise, the method sets the value of the isPINValid property to true.

```
    isPINValid = true
    print("PIN OK")

}
```

Now let's have a look at the withdraw(amount:) method:

```
public func withdraw(amount: Float) -> Bool {
```

First, we check the isPINValid property; if the PIN is not valid, the method exits by returning false.

```
    guard isPINValid == true else {
        return false
    }
```

If the user entered a valid PIN, we perform a couple of validations: the amount should be a positive value, and we also check the balance before withdrawing the amount.

```
    print("> Withdraw $\(amount)")

    guard amount > 0 else {
        print("Error! Enter a valid amount")
        return false
    }

    var result = true

    if availableFunds >= amount {
        availableFunds -= amount
    } else {
        print("Insufficient funds!")
        result = false
    }

    print("Transaction Complete... don't forget your card!")
```

```
        return result
    }
```

Let's test our ATM simulator:

```
let atm = ATM()
atm.enter(pin: "1234")

atm.withdraw(amount: 500)
```

The program prints:

```
PIN OK
> Withdraw $500.0

Transaction Complete... don't forget your card!
```

This code works as expected; however, it's far from perfect. As we add new features, the complexity of the conditional logic keeps increasing.

```
if pinValid {
    //...
    if amount > 0 {
        //...
        if availableFunds >= amount {
            //...
        } else {
            //...
        }
    } else {
        //...
    }
} else {
    //...
}
```

In the next section, we address this problem using the State design pattern.

16.3 Solution: the State Pattern

In this section, we refactor the ATM class using the State design pattern. Our goal is to replace the conditional logic with dedicated states.

Start by defining the common interface for our states. The ATMState protocol is fileprivate to avoid exposing it to callers. This is the protocol that declares the functionality for all the concrete state types.

```
public final class ATM {
    // ...
}

fileprivate protocol ATMState {
```

We need methods for entering and validating the PIN. validate(pin:) takes a parameter of type String.

```
    func validate(pin: String)
```

We also need the method for withdrawing the money; withdraw(amount:) is marked as mutating because it may modify the internal state of value types. The method has a parameter called amount of type Float. The method returns a Bool value that indicates if the call was successful:

```
    mutating func withdraw(amount: Float) -> Bool
```

Let's also add a method to mark the end of the transaction.

```
    func transactionCompleted(success: Bool)
```

Next, we provide default behavior using a protocol extension.

```
extension ATMState {
    func validate(pin: String) {
        print("\(#function) not implemented for \(self) state")
    }

    mutating func withdraw(amount: Float) -> Bool {
        print("\(#function) not implemented for \(self) state")
        return false
    }

    func transactionCompleted(success: Bool) {
        print("\(#function) not implemented for \(self) state")
    }
}
```

The concrete state types should only implement the functionality they are responsible for. For the rest, the default implementation will be invoked. The default implementations don't do anything meaningful; they print messages to the console stating that the method is not implemented for the given type.

Now let's start defining the concrete states.

Note that all the state types and the `ATMState` protocol are fileprivate. That's required because we don't want clients to interact with the states directly. They should only be able to work with instances of the `ATM` class.

We start with the `IdleState` type:

```
fileprivate struct IdleState: ATMState {}
```

This state does nothing, as it represents the ATM's idle state.

The next state is the `EnterPINState`.

```
fileprivate struct EnterPINState: ATMState {
```

There are different ways to implement the State pattern. We could embed the state changes in the `ATM` class. Another approach is to let the state types handle the state transitions.

We're going to use the second approach to keep our `ATM` class clean and simple. For this, the state needs to access the `ATM` instance—also known as context—to change its state. We declare a `context` property of type `ATM`.

```
fileprivate struct EnterPINState: ATMState {
    var context: ATM
```

The `EnterPINState` type implements the `validate(pin:)` method.

```
    func validate(pin: String) {
```

The method performs a simple PIN validation. If the PIN is invalid, we print a message to the console and stop the process.

```
        guard pin == "1234" else {
            print("INVALID PIN")
```

We need a new state to mark the end of the transaction—let's call it `TransactionCompleteState`. The context property has to update its state. This state is going to implement the `transactionCompleted(success:)` method.

```
            context.state = TransactionCompleteState(context: con-
```

```
text)
                context.state.transactionCompleted(success: false)
                return
        }
        print("PIN OK")
        context.state = WithdrawState(context: context)
    }
```

Here's the implementation of the `TransactionCompleteState` type:

```
fileprivate struct TransactionCompleteState: ATMState {
    var context: ATM

    func transactionCompleted(success: Bool) {
```

I compose a message based on the `success` parameter and print it to the console.

```
        var statusMessage = success ? "Transaction complete..." :
"Transaction failed..."
        statusMessage += " don't forget your card!"
        print(statusMessage)
```

And finally, we need to update the state of the context to `IdleState`.

```
        context.state = IdleState()
    }
}
```

The `ATM` class has no `state` property yet. So, let's define it:

```
public final class ATM {
    fileprivate var state: ATMState = IdleState()
    // ...
}
```

Now go back to the `EnterPINState validate(pin:)` method:

```
fileprivate struct EnterPINState: ATMState {
    // ...
    func validate(pin: String) {
        guard pin == "1234" else {
            // ...
            return
        }
```

If the PIN entry was successful, we should allow the user to withdraw the money.

```
        print("PIN OK")
        context.state = WithdrawState(context: context)
    }
}
```

We need to add another state. `WithdrawState` conforms to the `ATMState` protocol. In addition to the context property, let's add the `availableFunds` property. We'll use it to check the balance:

```
fileprivate struct WithdrawState: ATMState {
    var context: ATM
    var availableFunds: Float = 1000

    init(context: ATM) {
        self.context = context
    }
}
```

The `WithdrawState` type implements the `withdraw(amount:)` method.

```
    mutating func withdraw(amount: Float) -> Bool {
        print("> Withdraw $\(amount)")
```

If the amount is negative or there are not sufficient funds, we switch the context's state to `TransactionCompleteState`. Then, we call the state's `transactionCompleted(success:)` method with the success argument set to `false`. This call will then change the ATM's state to `IdleState`.

```
        guard amount > 0 else {
            print("Error! Enter a valid amount")
            context.state = TransactionCompleteState(context: con-
text)
            context.state.transactionCompleted(success: false)
            return false
        }

        guard availableFunds >= amount else {
            print("Insufficient funds!")
            context.state = TransactionCompleteState(context: con-
text)
            context.state.transactionCompleted(success: false)
            return false
        }
```

If we pass the validation steps, we simply subtract the amount from the available funds. Then, we switch the context's state to `TransactionCompleteState`. Finally, let's mark the transaction as successfully completed by calling the `transactionCompleted(success:)` method with the success argument set to `true`.

```
        availableFunds -= amount
        context.state = TransactionCompleteState(context: context)
        context.state.transactionCompleted(success: true)
        return true
    }
}
```

Now we can refactor the ATM class too, so let's remove the obsolete parts. The old properties have become useless, so delete them:

```
public final class ATM {
    // private var isPINValid = false
    // private var availableFunds: Float = 1000
```

Next, revamp the `enter(pin:)` method. We replace the old implementation with the following code:

```
    public func enter(pin: String) {
        state = EnterPINState(context: self)
        state.validate(pin: pin)
    }
```

We set the ATM's state to `EnterPINState` and call the state's `validate(pin:)` method.

Next comes the `withdraw(amount:)` method.

```
    public func withdraw(amount: Float) -> Bool {
        // invoke withdraw(amount:) on a copy
        // of the state property to prevent
        // memory access exclusivity* violations
        var stateCopy = state
        return stateCopy.withdraw(amount: amount)
    }
```

The feature called "exclusive access to memory" was introduced a while back, but as of Swift 5 it gets enforced by the compiler. You can read about it here: https://swift.org/blog/swift-5-exclusivity/.

When clients call this method, the ATM instance should be in the `WithdrawState`. This is the only state that implements the `withdraw(amount:)` method. The other states will fall back to the default behavior that simply prints a log message.

All right, we're done with the refactoring work. Get ready to test our solution.

```
let atm = ATM()
atm.enter(pin: "1234")
atm.withdraw(amount: 500)
```

The output will be:

```
PIN OK
> Withdraw $500.0
Transaction Complete… don't forget your card!
```

Everything works just as before. However, the current design is entirely different.

We removed all the conditional logic from the ATM class. Instead of having code like:

```
if pinValid {
    //...
    if amount > 0 {
        //...
        if availableFunds >= amount {
            //...
        } else {
            //...
        }
    } else {
        //...
    }
} else {
    //...
}
```

We have dedicated states that perform the required logic and trigger the state changes:

→ IdleState

→ EnterPINState

→ WithdrawState

→ TransactionCompleteState

This approach produces a more flexible design and lets us easily add new states and state transitions.

16.4 Conclusion

The State design pattern allows objects to behave differently as their internal state changes. It can be applied successfully to remove monolithic conditional logic from a software system.

To implement the State pattern, you need to identify the steps that cause changes in the behavior of an object. Then, extract these steps and incorporate them into dedicated State types.

The state types should be used exclusively by the context. Clients should interact with the interface provided by the context.

17. WHAT'S NEXT?

17.1 Congrats!

You've reached the end of this book!

By now, you've probably become familiar with the battle-proven best practices and principles known as software design patterns.

To apply them successfully in your upcoming projects, you'll need to practice a lot. I suggest you start exploring these design patterns by implementing smaller demos first. Swift Playground projects are a great place to experiment.

And if you found this book useful, please leave a nice review at https://www.amazon.com/gp/product/B07MDD3FQJ.

Thank you!

17.2 Useful Links

As an instructor, my goal is to share my 25+ years of software development expertise.

My books are available on Amazon amazon.com/author/nyisztor and iTunes https://itunes.apple.com/us/author/karoly-nyisztor/id1345964804?mt=11.

Check out my courses on:

- → Teachable: https://learnwithkarl.teachable.com
- → Udemy: https://www.udemy.com/user/karolynyisztor/
- → LinkedIn Learning: https://www.linkedin.com/learning/instructors/karoly-nyisztor?u=2125562
- → Pluralsight: https://www.pluralsight.com/profile/author/karoly-nyisztor

Check out these links for free tutorials, blog posts, and other useful stuff:

- → https://www.leakka.com
- → https://www.youtube.com/@LearnWithKarl
- → https://github.com/nyisztor
- → https://x.com/knyisztor

www.ingramcontent.com/pod-product-compliance
Lightning Source LLC
Chambersburg PA
CBHW021816170526
45157CB00007B/2604